# THE STORY OF
# MUSIC

## VOLUME 3

## Music from
## Around the World

GROLIER
EDUCATIONAL

# ABOUT THIS BOOK

This book is one of a set of ten that tells the story of music from earliest times to the present day. Starting with the primitive sounds made by the crude instruments devised by early human beings, the first book traces the development of music through the centuries, describing how it evolved and how musical instruments became more refined and ever more capable of delivering beautiful sounds. The second book in the series focuses on the music of the 19th and 20th centuries, showing how the orchestra developed to become the impressively large body that it is today, and how composers ranged through a variety of musical styles, culminating in the exciting electronic experiments of the late 20th century.

Other volumes in the series look at music from around the world and U.S. music in the forms of folk, country, and Cajun, as well as gospel, blues, and jazz. A whole volume examines modern music, from rock 'n' roll to hip-hop. Another book looks at musicals, operetta, and film music, while music education and the music business are also given an entire volume. A whole book focuses on musical instruments and recording technology, while the final book in the series looks at the voice, opera, songs, and singing in general.

The books are fully illustrated, and each volume ends with a timeline, a glossary of musical terms and notation, a list of further reading, and a comprehensive index covering the complete set.

Published 2001 by Grolier Educational
Sherman Turnpike
Danbury, Connecticut 06816

© 2001 Brown Partworks Ltd

Set ISBN: 0-7172-9559-1
Volume ISBN: 0-7172-9562-1

Library of Congress Cataloging-in-Publication Data
Story of music
   p. cm.
   Includes indexes.
   Contents: v. 1. Classical music from earliest times -- v. 2. Classical music: romantic to modern -- v. 3. Music from around the world -- v. 4. Folk, country, and cajun music -- v. 5. Gospel, blues, and jazz - - v. 6. From rock and pop to hip-hop -- v. 7. Music of stage and screen -- v. 8. The music profession -- v. 9. Musical instruments and technology -- v. 10. The voice and song.
   ISBN 0-7172-9559-1 (set: alk. paper) -- ISBN 0-7172-9560-5 (v. 1: alk. paper) -- ISBN 0-7179-9561-3 (v. 2: alk. paper) -- ISBN 0-7172-9562-1 (v. 3: alk. paper) -- ISBN 0-7172-9563-X (v. 4: alk. paper) -- ISBN 0-7172-9564-8 (v. 5: alk. paper) -- ISBN 0-7172-9565-6 (v. 6: alk. paper) -- ISBN 0-7172-9566-4 (v. 7: alk. paper) -- ISBN 0-7172-9567-2 (v. 8: alk. paper) -- ISBN 0-7172-9568-0 (v. 9: alk. paper) -- ISBN 0-7172-9569-9 (v. 10: alk. paper)
   1. Music--History and criticism--Juvenile literature. [Music--History and criticism.]
ML3928 .S76 2000
780--dc21
                                                    00-023220

For information address the publisher:
Grolier Educational, Sherman Turnpike,
Danbury, Connecticut 06816

Printed in Singapore

**Glossary**
Words that are explained in the glossary are printed in **bold** type the first time they appear in a chapter.

FOR BROWN PARTWORKS LTD

Editor:             Julian Flanders
Deputy editor:      Sally McFall
Design:             Kelly-Anne Levey
Picture research:   Helen Simm

Managing editor:    Lindsey Lowe
Production:         Matt Weyland

Contributor:        Jeff Kaliss
Consultant:         Daniel Ferguson

PHOTOGRAPHIC CREDITS
Front cover: African drummer, **Still Pictures**.
Title page: Trinidad carnival, **Corbis**, Pablo Corral V.
**AFP:** 49br; **Archive Photos:** Frank Driggs 13, Deborah Feingold 14; **Arena Images:** John Fenton 52tr, Ronald Grant Archive 18, 37b, Jak Kilby 19t, 22t, 35, 43b, 45b, 48, 53t, 55, 56t, 59, 60t&b, 62, 63 b, 65t&b, Eric Richmond 37t, Colin Willoughby 6tc; **Adrian Boot:** 36, 41br; **Robin Broadbank:** 27br; **Corbis:** 29br, Archivo Iconografico 24tr, Tiziana and Gianni Baldizzone 25, Jan Butchofsky/Houser 39, Bettmann 11br, Richard Bickell 17b, 23tl, 41tl, Pablo Corral V 32, Sergio Dorantes 20, Ken Franckling 16tl, Mitchell Gerber 15br, Phillip Gould 34b; Daniel Laine 4, 38bc, David Lees 54, Catherine Karnow 47tl, Stephanie Maze 11tl, 28, Charles O'Rear 66b, Christine Osborne 50, Richard Pasley 22br, Reuters Newmedia Inc 15tc, 19br, UPI 15tl; **Sylvia Cordaiy Photo Library:** Julian Worker 49tl; **Mary Evans Picture Library:** 10, 33, Steve Rumney 30br; **Hulton Getty:** 5tr, 7br, 12, 21, 23bc, 29tl, 38tr, 45tc, 57; **The Kobal Collection:** 27tl; **The Lebrecht Collection:** 46t&b, David Farrell 43tl, J Highet 8tr, 56bl, Odile Noel 44, G Salter 40, Chris Stock 5bc, 8br, 24bc, 52bl; **Naomi Mori:** 53br; **Panos Pictures:** Giacomo Pirozzi 58; **Papilio Photographic:** 51; **Pictorial Press Ltd:** 63tl; **Redferns:** Chris van der Vooren 67; **Rex Features:** 31; **South American Pictures:** Rolando Pujol 7tl, 17tr; **Still Pictures:** Julio Etchart 9, John Isaac 42, Margaret Wilson 64.
Page 15b courtesy Fania Records, page 26t&c courtesy Tumi (Music) Ltd, page 30t courtesy Monitor Records, page 34t courtesy Ace Records Ltd, page 47b courtesy Island Records, page 61 courtesy Shanachie Records (photo Nicolas Segalen), page 66t courtesy Virgin Records.
**Key:** b=below, t=top, c=center, l=left, r=right.
Every effort has been made to trace copyright holders and gain permission for material reproduced in this volume. We regret if any errors have occurred.

Maps and artworks: Colin Woodman
Musical notation: Harry Boteler

# Contents

## VOLUME 3

## Music from Around the World

CHAPTER 1

# The Sound of Salsa

The word "salsa" was coined in the 1970s to describe a fiery dance music that had its roots in Cuba and Puerto Rico as far back as the 15th century. After blazing through Latin America and the U.S., it is now becoming popular all over the world.

Salsa is a Spanish word that means "sauce." The word can be seen on restaurant menus, but since the 1970s it has also been the name for a catchy type of dance music that had its roots in Cuba and Puerto Rico. Spreading beyond these two islands to other places in the Caribbean and Latin America, the music eventually reached the cities of New York and Miami, where there are many Cuban and Puerto Rican emigrants.

As the name suggests, salsa music can be as tasty as a dish of Cuban *ropa vieja* (steak in spicy tomato sauce). It has been used to spice up TV advertisements and movie soundtracks, and to get people of all kinds and ages dancing in schools, festivals, nightclubs, and elsewhere.

**Above: A woman dances on the streets of Havana, Cuba, to the rhythms of a rumba band. Rumba had a great influence on the development of salsa.**

## Salsa roots

The roots of salsa, of course, reach farther back than the 1970s. Salsa came from the musics of the Spanish explorers and settlers who started to arrive in the Caribbean in the 15th century, and from the Africans whom they brought over as slaves to work the fields, mines, and towns of the so-called New World. Even the French added their **rhythms** to this spicy musical sauce when they arrived from the neighboring island of Saint Domingue in the 18th century. Yet long before the first Spanish and their black slaves arrived, Arawak Indians lived on the Caribbean islands. Unfortunately, they were mostly killed off by the diseases, hard work, and weapons that came with the new settlers. The Arawaks did, however, leave behind a couple of musical instruments that are still used in salsa: the maracas—made from gourds, which are the dried and hollowed-out shells of a squash, filled with seeds to make a swishing sound when shaken—and the guiro, a gourd with deep notches cut into it that makes a scratchy, clicking sound when scraped with a stick.

Most of the other percussion instruments, along with the hip-shaking rhythms in salsa, came with the African slaves and developed over the course of two and a half centuries. The slaves were not allowed to carry much with them from their own countries; but after arriving in the islands, they were able to recreate a number of the drums they had left behind in West and Central Africa, including the tall conga and the hourglass-shaped *bata*. They also had the *shekere* (a rattle made from a gourd), the

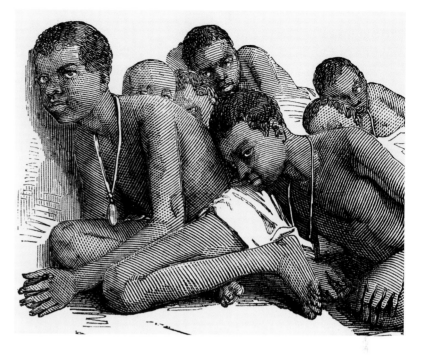

**Above: Slaves had almost no room to move on the boats that carried them from Africa, and even sleeping conditions were very difficult.**

**Below: Claves were introduced by the Africans and are an instrument often used to set the main rhythm in salsa.**

*guagua* (a wooden tube), and the claves—wooden blocks that make a clear, almost bell-like sound when they are banged together.

## Cuban beginnings

By the 1840s Africans made up nearly half the Cuban population. By the time slavery was abolished in Cuba in 1873, almost one million Africans had been taken to Cuba as slaves. Their Spanish masters had forced most of them to adopt the Catholic religion, but the slaves never fully abandoned their own African religions, which involved the worship of several gods based on nature and human activity. Their saints, called orishas, included Chango—the spirit of fire and war—and Oshun, the goddess of love and water. The slaves' devotion to both African and Christian gods became known as the Santería religion.

Much of the music of **rumba** (see pages 6–7), which existed before salsa and greatly influenced it, came from religious prayers and celebrations. Rumba also goes back to African mating dances, which encouraged the connection between men and women and the making of families.

The Spanish influence in salsa can be easily seen and heard in the many stringed instruments that are used to play it. They include the Cuban *tres*, which is a type of guitar that has three sets of double strings; the Puerto Rican *cuatro*, with five sets of double strings (see page 11); and of course the familiar six-stringed guitar (see right). They all developed from instruments taken to Spain more than a thousand years ago by the Moors, who came from the Middle East and invaded Spain and northern Africa (see page 55). The Moorish influence can also be heard in the haunting melodies, favoring the **minor modes**, which were carried by the Spanish to the New World. A good example of one of these modes is the Phrygian. It is made up of a **scale** where the semitones fall between the first and second and fifth and sixth notes. When it is played, it creates a feeling of sadness; but the words of many Cuban songs that use this mode are happy ones.

**Below: The Spanish brought their classical guitar to the musical mix of salsa.**

**Below: The sad-sounding Phrygian mode can be played on the white notes of a keyboard by playing a scale of E, F, G, A, B, C, D, E, as written below.**

The French contribution to salsa is the *contradanza*, which means "counter dance." It started out in the 17th century as an English country dance in which the dancers stood "counter" or opposite one another. By the end of the 17th century it had become popular with the French as contredanse and was performed at formal occasions as a slow dance to wind down the evening after faster dances like the **minuet**. On the French Caribbean island of Saint Domingue—which is now divided into two countries called the Dominican Republic and Haiti—African rhythms were added to the contredanse, influenced by the African slaves there, and it became the favorite type of music and dance on the island throughout the 18th century. In 1791 a political revolution on Saint Domingue caused many French noble families to flee with their servants to Cuba's east coast, taking contredanse with them. As it was added to Cuban music, it was renamed *contradanza cubana*, later shortened to *contradanza*.

**Cuba's musical forms**

Many different musical forms have been added to the melting pot of salsa over the years. In fact, several of them may show up in any one performance or recording. To understand the flavors in salsa's tasty sauce, it is important to know all the ingredients.

One of the oldest forms used in Cuban salsa is rumba. Rumba uses a particular African rhythm called the clave—pronounced "kla-vey" and translated as "key." The clave is sometimes played at the beginning of a song by the instrument of the same name—the wooden blocks called claves (see page 5). By banging the claves together, the rhythm can be counted out as 1-2-3, 1-2-and-1-2-3,

**Phrygian Mode**

6

Left: These street musicians in Havana are playing many of the instruments found in rumba bands: the barrel-shaped conga drums, the square box drums called *cajones*, and the *shekere*—a rattle made from a gourd.

1-2, slightly delaying the second beat in each group of three. This is known as the three-two clave beat. A similar, but reversed, beat is known as the two-three clave. These two types of clave beats underpin the rhythm of all salsa or Latin music and give it its characteristic swing. Other percussion instruments then set up **cross-rhythms** (conflicting rhythms, such as two notes played against three notes) or **polyrhythms** (different rhythms played at the same time) against the clave rhythm.

Rumbas are led by a lead singer, called the *akpwón*, who sets the **pitch** for the rumba by singing the opening line unaccompanied. Once he has set the pitch, the clave rhythm begins, and the group of singers add their voices to the thundering beat. The *akpwón* sings solo, and the group sings in **chorus** in a back-and-forth pattern called "call and response." Specific dance patterns are also performed. The main instruments of rumba are the conga drums and tuned wooden boxes, accompanied by percussion such as guiros and claves.

Rumba came from African rhythms taken over by the slaves and developed on the docks of Havana and Matanzas. The first rumbas were played on packing cases because the

slaves had not been allowed to bring their drums with them from Africa. They discovered that different-sized packing cases sounded different **tones** when hit—codfish cases sounded a low tone, while candle boxes made a high tone. Today rumba players use specially made boxes called *cajones*,

Below: Two rumba dancers in full swing as they perform the dance for spectators in Cuba.

which include the *tumbadora* (the bass tone), the *segunda* (the middle tone), and the *quinto* (the high tone).

There are three main rhythms used in rumba—the *guaguancó*, the *yambu*, and the *columbia*. The *guaguancó* accompanies a fast dance between a man and woman that acts out the gestures of a rooster and a hen (see picture on page 7, bottom right). The *yambu* rhythm has a Spanish influence and accompanies a smooth, slow dance in which the couple act out two old people with their shuffling movements. The *columbia*, the most African of the rumba rhythms, is a fast dance for a single male performer to show off, and in which he resembles a strutting peacock.

## Parent of salsa

The Cuban musical form of *son*—pronounced like "sown" and meaning "sound"—is known as the parent of salsa because it is the basis of all Cuban music, combining African drum rhythms with Spanish poetry and guitar melodies. Like rumba, *son* is based on the clave rhythm (see pages 6–7), but there are more players in a *son* band than in a rumba band, and the musical **arrangements** are usually more complex.

*Son* developed in Oriente, the eastern region of Cuba, and later blossomed in different areas of the island, including Havana. The first *son* song was probably "Má Teodora"—about a slave and her sister who sang around Santiago in the 1550s. But *son* really began to take off when Cuba won the War of Independence with Spain in 1868, and the new spirit of freedom found expression in music.

The first *son* instruments were guitar, claves, and maracas. In time, other instruments were added, including more guitars, *tres* (see page 6), double bass, and *marímbula*—a wooden box with metal prongs that are plucked by a leather strap. Finally, in the mid-1920s the trumpet and bongo—a small set of drums held in the lap and played with the flat of the hand—were added. The melody of *son* is usually played by guitar and *tres*. The singer, who must have a strong **tenor** voice, sings about everything from love to local or political events. *Son* went through many changes in the 20th century, absorbing other musical forms such as jazz and pop, and adding many of the instruments used by European and U.S. bands.

**Above:** This informal *son* band shows instruments often used in *son* music. The musician in front plays the cowbell and bongo drums. Behind him is a *shekere*—a gourd rattle covered by a net of threaded beads that is both struck and shaken.

**Below:** Maracas are one of the main instruments of salsa.

## Cuba's country music

While *son* is considered to be Cuba's folk music, *musica campesina* is its country music. In fact, *musica campesina* is Spanish for "country music." It is melodic and emotional, with gentle rhythms, and the **lyrics** are long and sometimes funny stories about the beauty of women and nature or about historical or political events. The voice used in *musica campesina* is high-pitched and is always accompanied by guitar and another stringed instrument. This second instrument is often the *laoud*—the Cuban version of the Arabic oud, which was brought over by the Spanish (see Volume 1, page 26). Otherwise, it is the *tres* guitar or the *bandurria*, which is similar to the mandolin. *Musica campesina* was developed by the many different nationalities that lived in the Cuban countryside—African sugar-cane workers, Canary Island tobacco growers, Cuban gauchos (cowboys), and Spanish peasant farmers.

## From *contradanza* to *danzón*

After the French settlers arrived in Cuba with the contredanse and it became known as the *contradanza*, it went through many changes as it was mixed with other forms of Cuban music. At first it was an instrumental music played by a band. The melody was mainly played by the violin and brass instruments, and the rhythm was played by two thundering timpani drums. The *contradanza* was later spiced up and became the *danza*, which was faster and more melodic.

Then, at a New Year's Party in 1879 in Mantanzas Province, a bandleader named Miguel Failde (1852–1899) played a melody that was announced as a *danzón*. He had taken the *danza*, slowed it down, and broken it into three parts, separated by a pause. This pause is an important feature of the *danzón*, since the dancers also pause at this moment in the music, usually when they are in a close embrace. He also introduced two new sections—a clarinet solo and a trumpet solo—and a more upbeat rhythm. The dance became one performed by couples, rather than by individuals in a line.

In 1910 José Urfe (1879–1957), a clarinet player from Havana, added two more sections to the *danzón*: a cornet—which is a type of trumpet—solo and a vocal and chorus (call-and-response) section, both ideas that are

# OLD-STYLE SALSA LIVES

Some of Cuba's musicians continue to play the older styles of salsa, such as *son*, rumba, and *musica campesina*. The group Los Muñequitos de Matanzas, which started in 1952, performs rumba with mainly traditional percussion but no horns and features dancers dressed in African costume. The singer Celina González (b. 1928), who is also from Matanzas Province east of Havana, began performing a country music version of *son* with her husband Reutilio Dominquez on guitar or bongos. After her husband's death in 1971 González continued performing but added trumpet and more percussion to her music. Although she has toured the Caribbean and New York, González remains a citizen of Cuba, where her regional *son* is enjoyed and appreciated much in the same way that country and western music is in North America.

Above: The Cuban country singer Celina González in concert.

SO NEAR AND YET SO FOREIGN
90 Miles from Key West

ViSiT CUBA

**Above: A tourist poster from the 1930s attempts to lure visitors from Miami to Cuba with the attractive image of a salsa dancer playing the maracas.**

violins and flute. Now all *son* that uses violin and flute is called *charanga*. *Danzón* is loved by older Cubans, although it has little in the way of African **syncopation**—when a note or chord is accented on a "weak" beat rather than on a strong beat such as the first or third. The trombone, with its low melancholy tone, is a key instrument in the *danzón*.

### Puerto Rican forms

The French contredanse also influenced the music of Puerto Rico. It arrived on the island around the middle of the 19th century and, as in Cuba, it was spiced up by local rhythms and called the *danza*. It was originally a very slow-tempo dance, so that the dancers could perform it without sweating, but later it became faster, with a more military feel. One of the first *danzas* to have lyrics was the Puerto Rican national **anthem**, "*La Borinqueña*" ("The Puerto Rican Girl"). It was written in 1868 during an uprising against the Spanish who then ruled the island. Yet the first *danzas* recorded, in 1910, were instrumentals that used a brass band and a small orchestra of stringed instruments and piano.

As in Cuba, many of the musical forms in Puerto Rico came from the African slaves who were brought to the island. One of the oldest of these forms is called *bomba*. *Bomba* music has a strong, driving rhythm with a syncopated lurch in the beat. The main rhythm is played on drums shaped like wooden barrels, also called *bombas*, with smaller drums (called *subidors*), maracas, and wooden sticks (*palillos*) creating cross-rhythms. Singers add to the rhythms by imitating the drums, while the dancers form a circle in front of the drummers. As the music builds, one of the dancers moves out of the circle

used in *son* (see page 8). He also introduced an even faster **tempo**. In 1930 the pianist and composer Antonio María Romeu (1876–1955) was at a party in Havana and jumped up to play with the band on a *danzón* "to liven it up a bit." From then on, the piano became an important instrument in the *danzón*. Romeu also created a type of *danzón* he called *charanga francesa* by taking out the brass instruments and adding

**Left: This guitar-maker in his shop in Utado, Puerto Rico, is holding a *cuatro* guitar—an instrument often used in salsa.**

**Below: The slums of Ponce in Puerto Rico, where the musical form of *plena* developed, were named *La Joya del Castillo* ("The Jewel of the Castle") by residents who enjoyed a joke.**

played with a **pick**. There are two styles of *jibaro*: *seis* and *aguinaldo*. *Seis* songs are complex and are written in either *décimas* or free form. The *aguinaldo* is the Puerto Rican Christmas carol, performed by singing groups who go from house to house, where they are given food and rum.

### Jewel from the ghetto

The other main Puerto Rican musical form is the *plena*. It was brought to Ponce by an English family of street performers who came from either St. Kitts or Barbados at the end of the 19th century. The father, John Clarke, and mother, Catherine George, wrote and sang songs, accompanying themselves with guitar and tambourine, while their daughter Carolina played the *pandereta*—a tambourine without jingles. The lyrics were usually amusing or meaningful stories about life in Ponce's black

toward the drummers and dances a solo that influences the drummers' rhythms. The centers of *bomba* were the coastal towns of Ponce in the south and Loiza Aldea in the north. Slaves, when they were allowed out on Christian holidays, would come flooding in from the countryside for all-night *bomba* sessions in the town.

Another form of music influenced by African slaves is *musica jibara*. Like Cuba's *musica campesina*, it is Puerto Rico's country music. It was created by a combination of escaped African slaves and Spanish peasant farmers who lived in mountain villages—the word *jibaro* means "those who escape civilization." The lyrics are usually about country life and are written in verses of 10 lines, called *décimas*. The songs are accompanied by the bongo, guiro, and the *cuatro*—a Puerto Rican four-stringed guitar, which later became a five-double-stringed guitar,

ghetto, which was sarcastically known as *La Joya del Castillo* ("The Jewel of the Castle"). The family's music was soon influenced by the local rhythms and became very popular there, where it was called *plena*. Later, *plena* was made popular outside of Ponce by Joselino Oppenheimer, who was also known as "Bumbún." Although he lived in *La Joya*, he worked as a plowman in the sugar-cane fields in the countryside, where he taught his *plena* songs to fellow workers. As he sang, he accompanied himself on drums, while other musicians played guiro, *pandereta*, and the accordion

## The folk music form of plena *is Puerto Rico's version of Cuban* son

or harmonica. He added a double-beat rhythm (played twice as fast as a normal beat), which became known as bum-bun. This rhythm was played by the *pandereta*, and this instrument and the accordion soon became the main ones for the *plena*. Later additions to the *plena* band were the double bass and the *cuatro* guitar.

The *plena* is Puerto Rico's version of *son* (see page 8). By the start of the 20th century many music forms were beginning to cross over from Cuba to Puerto Rico and vice versa, creating a more international salsa brew.

### Introducing the mambo

In both Cuba and Puerto Rico the old musical forms began to be updated by 20th-century composers. A good example of this is the mambo. It emerged out of the *danzón* form to become one of the most popular rhythms of salsa. Mambo is a musical form driven by a **funky** African-type

rhythm. No one knows for sure who invented it, but it is likely to have been the flute player Antonio Arcano (b. 1911). Arcano had one of the most popular *danzón* orchestras in Cuba in the 1930s, called Las Maravillas del Siglo ("The Miracles of the Century"). The band's rhythm was driven by three brothers—Cachao Lopez (b. 1918) on double bass, Jesús Lopez on cello, and Orestes Lopez (b. 1908) on piano. In 1938 Orestes wrote some music he called "Mambo," influenced by Cachao's bass rhythm, and tacked it on to the end of a *danzón*. Arcano called this new music *nuevo ritmo*—the "new rhythm." To strengthen this rhythm, he added percussion instruments like the cowbell (a metal bell similar to those that are hung around the necks

**Above: Cuban bandleader and piano player Perez Pantalon Prado (1916–1989) demonstrates the cha-cha-cha in Paris, France. There are a few who credit Prado with inventing the mambo, and there is certainly no doubt that he had some huge international hits with mambo songs in the 1940s.**

of cows in the countryside, which is hit with a drum stick), conga, and timbales (a pair of drums played while standing) to the traditional *charanga* instruments. The *nuevo ritmo* mambo was banned by Havana radio stations for six months after its invention and was never very popular in Cuba, yet within five years people all over the world were dancing to it.

The mambo is generally fast and rhythmic; but when slowed down and simplified, it becomes known as the cha-cha-cha. The cha-cha-cha was invented in 1953 by the violinist Enrique Jorrin (1926–1987) in his song "*La Engañadora*" ("The Deceiver"), about a woman he had seen on the streets of Havana. He named this music the cha-cha-cha from the sound the dancers' feet made as they moved to its rhythm. Both the mambo and the cha-cha-cha are slightly syncopated, but not too fast. When they were introduced to U.S. popular music both the mambo and cha-cha-cha became instant dance crazes.

## Salsa comes to the U.S.

Along with the introduction of certain styles of Caribbean music to the U.S. have come several waves of people from Cuba and Puerto Rico, particularly into New York City. Like most immigrants, Cubans and Puerto Ricans believed they could find better jobs and a higher standard of living there. Musicians such as Mario Bauzá (1911–1993) and Frank "Machito" Grillo (1909–1984) from Havana, who had become fans of the American **swing** music they

Below: Mario Bauzá helped create a new style of music called Latin jazz by being one of the first musicians to bring Cuban rhythms to U.S. jazz music.

listened to on the radio and on recordings, joined U.S. big bands in the 1930s and 1940s.

However, when Cuban musicians joined U.S. bands, they also began to influence the music. Latin jazz was born when Cuban rhythms were added to the music of U.S. swing bands led by such legends as Chick Webb (1909–1939), Duke Ellington (1899–1974), and Cab Calloway (1907–1994). In 1935 Mario Bauzá was the musical director for the Chick Webb Orchestra, fronted by singer Ella Fitzgerald (1917–1996), while the band was performing regularly at the Savoy Ballroom in New York City.

Another band performing at the Savoy at the time was that of the Cuban flute player Alberto Socarras (1908–1987), who had recently hired U.S. jazz trumpeter Dizzy Gillespie (1917–1993) to give his Cuban music a more American sound.

Bauzá and Gillespie met there and became friends. When Webb died, they both joined Calloway's orchestra, introducing some Cuban rhythms and sowing the first seeds of what later became known as Latin jazz. By 1940 they had both left the band.

Gillespie then started his own band and hired Cuban percussionist Chano Pozo (1915–1948), who had been introduced to him by Bauzá. The combination of Pozo's drumming and Gillespie's trumpet playing caused a sensation, with jazz melodies being supported and driven along by the insistent Latin rhythms of the drums. In turn, Bauzá and his brother-in-law Machito started their own Latin jazz band called the Afro-Cubans and released a song called "Tanga" in 1943, which became a blueprint for the music. Other big-name Cuban bandleaders, including drummer Tito Puente (1923–2000) and piano

13

player Eddie Palmieri (b. 1936), emerged later, each strengthening and adding something to the Latin style. Puente was a **virtuoso** (master musician) on the timbales, while Palmieri gave the trombones an important role—using them to give melodic weight to the mambo—and added his own exciting style of piano playing, which used huge crashing chords to punctuate the rhythm.

## 1960s invasion

Another wave of emigration to New York and Miami came at the end of the Cuban dictatorship of Fulgencio Batista when communist Fidel Castro took power in 1959. Some musicians moved to the U.S. because they disagreed with the communists. Others left because of the dissolving of the U.S. tourist trade and lack of opportunities to record in Cuba—the island's only recording company is operated by its government.

Celia Cruz (b. 1924) is one of the salsa superstars who went to New York at this time. Cruz had already been a popular singer and film actress in Havana. She has worked with bandleaders such as Mario Bauzá, Tito Puente, Johnny Pacheco (b. 1935), and Willie Colón (b. 1950), who admired her skill at **improvising** around a melody and inventing new lyrics on the spot. This improvisation, an important part of all forms of salsa, echoes that used by singers in traditional African music, as well as that used by modern jazz instrumentalists and vocalists. Now in her seventies, Cruz still performs to big audiences worldwide.

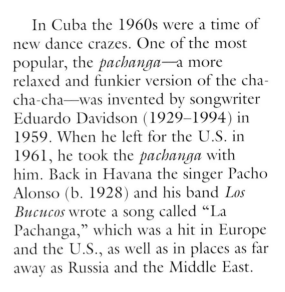

Below: Salsa singer Celia Cruz is known as the Queen of Salsa. With her warm voice and flamboyant style she arrived in New York in the 1960s and has been a worldwide success.

In Cuba the 1960s were a time of new dance crazes. One of the most popular, the *pachanga*—a more relaxed and funkier version of the cha-cha-cha—was invented by songwriter Eduardo Davidson (1929–1994) in 1959. When he left for the U.S. in 1961, he took the *pachanga* with him. Back in Havana the singer Pacho Alonso (b. 1928) and his band *Los Bucucos* wrote a song called "La Pachanga," which was a hit in Europe and the U.S., as well as in places as far away as Russia and the Middle East.

## Birth of "salsa"

By the 1970s generations of Cubans and Puerto Ricans living in New York and Miami had opened a number of dancehalls and nightclubs in which to enjoy their music. These clubs soon began to attract dancers from other backgrounds, even when they couldn't understand the Spanish lyrics. The musical arrangements had become more complex under the continuing influence of Latin jazz, and the louder and flashier percussion sounded more exciting on the dance floor than the old mambos and cha-cha-chas. This Latin music now became an alternative to **disco**—another hugely popular 1970s dance form, although rhythmically less interesting than salsa. It was during this period of increased popularity that Cuban and Puerto Rican music gained the new name of "salsa," though in fact many of its sounds and performers were not new at all.

Among the record companies that helped get salsa to the ears of its fans was Fania Records, based in Manhattan. Fania producers such as the Dominican Johnny Pacheco and

# PARTNERS IN SUCCESS

**Willie Colón has recorded some of salsa's most influential hit albums.**

**Rubén Blades wrote songs about city life that became anthems for young Latins.**

Willie Colón grew up in a Puerto Rican neighborhood in Brooklyn, New York, listening to both U.S. and Puerto Rican music. He took up composing and playing the trombone and by age 17 had recorded his first hit album, *El malo* ("The Bad Guy") with singer Héctor Lavoe (b. 1946), who later became one of salsa's most important vocalists. From that time on Colón's career never looked back. His music is adored by many for its catchy melodies, sung in the high-pitched lead vocal style of Puerto Rican *jibaros*, surrounded by smooth vocal **harmonies** and a tight, punchy horn section. His lush brassy arrangements have found their way into a number of records produced for artists on Fania Records, such as the singer Celia Cruz. But his greatest success came when he got together with the Panamanian singer Rubén Blades (b. 1948).

Blades (pronounced "Bla-dess") was born into a Cuban-St. Lucian musical family in Panama City—his mother was a well-known singer, and his father played the congas. Blades studied law at the University of Panama before moving to New York, where he got a job in the mailroom at Fania Records. In 1974 he joined the record company band, the Fania All Stars, singing alongside Lavoe, with Colón on trombone. This sparked a partnership that would produce a magnificent display of musical fireworks.

After Colón produced a solo record for Blades on Fania Records in 1977, called *Matiendo Mano* ("Feeling Up"), the two decided to record a joint album together. The result was *Siembra* ("Seed"), released on Fania in 1978, which would turn out to be the most successful salsa album for the next 20 years. In *Siembra* Blades replaced the usual light "party"

lyrics of many salsa songs with lyrics about the injustice and desperation of life in the Spanish-speaking ghettos of major cities. As a lawyer, Blades was well-aware of the social and political problems that Latin people experienced. Together, Colón and Blades have been accredited with starting the *nueva canción* ("new song") movement, which made salsa socially aware and musically modern.

To date, Colón has 11 Grammy award nominations and 15 gold and five platinum albums to his name. He has worked with a number of musicians of other types of music, such as rock singer David Byrne (b. 1952), who has released records of Cuban music on his own Luaka Bop label. Colón has also appeared as a TV and film actor and become involved in politics, running for congress in 1994. Like Colón, Blades has been active in politics—running for the presidency of Panama (unsuccessfully)—and as an actor in several U.S. films, as well as on TV and Broadway.

In his later albums Blades added synthesizers and a full drum kit to the typical salsa instruments and bits of jazz, **doo-wop**, and rock to the typical salsa forms. He has also worked with rock artists such as Lou Reed (b. 1942) and Elvis Costello (b. 1955). Blades's charm, political commitment, and musical flexibility have made him one of the most popular performers of salsa music. The relationship between Cólon and Blades, although musically successful, was known to have been stormy. Yet the two reunited one more time in San Juan, Puerto Rico, in 1995, backed by Blades's band Son del Solar. Afterward they released an album called *Tras la tormenta* ("After the Storm").

**Right:** *Siembra* **by Colón and Blades was for many years salsa's best-selling album.**

and complex, and salsa was just being born. Several of Irakere's founding players have now left because they were unable to get U.S. citizenship or they achieved solo stardom as jazz musicians, but the band continues to work on the musical fusion of jazz and *son*. Los Van Van is perhaps closer to rock music. The group added electric guitars and **psychedelic** electronic keyboards to a traditional Cuban **lineup** of percussion, flute, violin, and horns, and called their new kind of sound "songo." Free to travel in the 1990s, Los Van Van became international dancehall favorites.

Puerto Rican Willie Colón, who were also both bandleaders and musicians, took care that salsa did not get stuck in one particular regional style. They made use of Cuban *son* and rumba (see pages 6–8), but also Puerto Rican *jibaros* and *plenas* (see pages 12-13), and Brazilian melodies.

**Above: Los Van Van perform with their own brand of U.S.-Cuban music they call "songo"—a popular mix that has brought them a string of hits.**

## Salsa sweeps the U.S.
The presence of Cubans and their music in the U.S. and Europe was again increased when Castro expelled 125,000 "undesirables" in 1981. In the late 1980s severe economic problems in the Dominican Republic also brought people from that Caribbean island to New York and Miami, where their quick, jumpy, Spanish-influenced dance music called **merengue**, led by the consistent beat of the güira, intermixed with salsa. Salsa's eagerness to embrace different regional and international styles has helped it find favor throughout the Spanish-speaking world—and beyond.

Two Cuban acts currently popular in the U.S. are Irakere and Los Van Van. Both started up in the late 1960s and early 1970s, when rock and jazz music were becoming more electrified

## U.S. havens of salsa
New York City still has the largest population of Cubans and Puerto Rican emigrants in the U.S., and therefore the greatest number of salsa clubs, some of which also cater to a recent return of interest in mambo (see pages 12–13). Salsa dancers spend a great deal of money on dance lessons and on fashions especially designed for

**Right: The singer Gloria Estefan grew up as a Cuban immigrant in Miami, Florida, and has brought salsa to the attention of millions of rock fans all over the world.**

the clubs. A new generation of salsa stars includes La India (b. 1969), whose high-pitched voice—sometimes rising in wild shrieks—and dramatic presence can whip her audience into a frenzy. Her 1998 album, *Sobre el fuego* ("On the Fire"), won a Grammy award nomination.

Miami and the neighboring areas of Miami Beach and Fort Lauderdale are home to many expatriates (former citizens of Cuba and Puerto Rico) and salsa fans, as well as to a major salsa record label, Guajiro. Yet there is much conflict in these Florida cities between older Cubans, who are bitter about everything that came after the Revolution, and younger Cubans, who are more accepting of whatever is danceable. The elder emigrants have sometimes opposed concerts by groups like Los Van Van because the performers still live in a communist country. Cuban-born rock star Gloria Estefan (b. 1957) shares the anti-Castro sentiments of her father, formerly a security guard for General Batista, but as vocalist for the Miami

Sound Machine, she helped salsa cross over to the American pop market with her 1985 hit "Conga."

## Cuba today

In Cuba *son* and rumba are officially supported by the government, but it is still hard to make a living by recording and performing on the island. Many Cuban towns and cities have a *casa de la trova*—a kind of community club where, long before the Revolution, *trovadores* (Spanish

**Above:** Cubans perform their music at a community center called a *casa de la trova* in Santiago, Cuba.

**Below:** A flashier show of salsa, with dazzling costumes and dancers, is seen at the *Tropicana*—a nightclub in Havana.

for "troubadours") gathered to sing their songs. Havana has two *casas*, but the most famous and active is at the opposite end of Cuba in Santiago.

Those that play in the *casas* are singer-songwriters who have adopted

## A CUBAN FAIRYTALE

Helping to fire up the Latin craze of the late 1990s was a group of musicians from Havana named the Buena Vista Social Club. When U.S. producer and guitarist Ry Cooder (b. 1947) and Nick Gold, the head of World Circuits Records, sought them out in Havana to make an album in 1996, the careers of most of these Cuban stars—including the singer Ibrahim Ferrer (b. 1926), pianist Rubén González (b. 1912), and the guitarist Compay Segundo (b. 1907)—seemed over. But the album they made together, entitled the *Buena Vista Social Club*, was such a huge international hit that it not only revitalized their careers, but suddenly made them into superstars. Soon they were playing sold-out shows in New York's Carnegie Hall and in major concert halls around the world, and their album won the Latin Grammy award in 1998. Though their music uses older song and dance forms, it appeals to fans of modern salsa, as well as to Americans who feel that they've just discovered Cuban music. The group's fame was enlarged on the big screen in a documentary filmed in Cuba by director Wim Wenders. Members of the group can also be heard on CD as part of the Afro Cuban All Stars, which also features some of Cuba's finest young players. *A Toda Cuba le Gusta* (1996) is a mix of old and new classics, while *Distinto, Diferente* (1999) features a big, brassy sound fronted by inspired vocals.

**Below: Guitarist Eliades Ochoa and singer Ibrahim Ferrer of The Buena Vista Social Club in a concert filmed by Wim Wenders.**

the *nueva trova* ("new **ballad**") style, called "new song" in the U.S. and *nueva canción* elsewhere in Latin America. It is an international movement of protest songs, with lyrics about global politics and injustices. Thanks to the relaxation of travel restrictions between Cuba and the U.S., more and more Americans are visiting the island, among them musicians, particularly from the world of jazz. Meanwhile, groups from Cuba have been playing to packed houses from Los Angeles to Boston.

### Salsa in Puerto Rico
Although Puerto Rico has added a great deal to salsa in the U.S., the music is harder to find on the streets of this island than on those of its Cuban neighbor. One of the few big salsa acts heard there and on tour abroad is El Gran Combo—a large band with a smoother, less syncopated sound than Cuban groups, which matches the smoother style of Puerto Rican dancing. This style may come from the island's strong Spanish influence—there have been far fewer Africans there than in Cuba. The spicy *bombas* and *plenas* are still popular in Puerto Rico, as is the folksy *jíbaro*, which is still a favorite in the countryside, much as country music is in North America.

### Other centers of salsa
Colombia and Venezuela, on the northern coast of South America, produce a salsa that is musically closer to Cuba than to Puerto Rico, even though they are farther away from Cuba geographically. Salsa musicians and fans in Colombia and Venezuela are close enough to the Caribbean to have picked up the music of Cuba and other island nations on their shortwave radios. The resulting mix can be heard in the sound of

performers like Joe Arroyo (b. 1955) and the singer-songwriter and bandleader Oscar D'León (b. 1943).

Joe Arroyo has become a salsa superstar with his own style, called Joe-son. It draws on merengue from the Dominican Republic, *compas* (a gentle, melodic, guitar-led music) from Haiti, **reggae** (a laid-back rhythm guitar and percussion music) from Jamaica, and *soca* from Trinidad (see page 41). These musical styles are mixed with *cumbia* (a type of music that has a gentle syncopated melody laid on top of a solid yet fiery beat) from Arroyo's own country of Colombia and the Cuban style of salsa. His stage shows with his band La Verdad ("The Truth") are spectacular both musically and visually, and feature his dancing and tough-sounding singing.

When not at home in Venezuela, the singer and bass player Oscar D'León appears often with his big band in New York and Miami. Like Arroyo, he has taken much from Cuban salsa arrangements for his 19-piece band and for his vocals. Salsa is wildly popular in Caracas, Venezuela's capital, although some local salsa bands show an influence

**Above: Colombian singer Joe Arroyo performs his own version of salsa called Joe-son with his band La Verdad.**

from the country's southern neighbor, Brazil, in the styles of **samba** and bossa nova (see page 28).

Salsa has now spread even further, as can be seen by visiting Salsaweb (http://www.salsaweb.com)—a site linking salsa activity in countries such as Spain, Sweden, Ivory Coast, India, Russia, and Korea. There seems to be no stopping the fiery beat of salsa.

## SALSA IN POP MUSIC

Salsa is becoming increasingly popular all over the world and has added its spicy flavor to some of the top acts in pop music. The U.S.-Puerto Rican salsa singer Ricky Martin (b. 1971) has had two huge hits with "La Copa de la Vida," the theme song for the 1998 World Cup, and "Livin' la Vida Loca" (1999). Even Madonna and the Spice Girls have had hits with pop songs that incorporate a salsa feel. This current trend of using salsa as an ingredient to spice up a pop song, along with the enormous success of groups like the Buena Vista Social Club and other performers of old-style salsa, prove that salsa is very much alive—in its many different forms.

**Right: Ricky Martin dances while singing his hit "Livin' la Vida Loca" at Miami Arena in October 1999.**

# CHAPTER 2

# Mexico and Latin America

Although they share a history of colonization by Spain and Portugal and have been influenced by European and U.S. music, Mexico and the countries of Latin America have developed a fascinating variety of their own styles of music.

Although Mexico is the closest Spanish-speaking neighbor of the U.S. (the common border is more than 2,000 miles long), the music of Mexico is largely unknown in most of the U.S., as well as in Europe and farther east. In the U.S, the most familiar type of Mexican music is mariachi because Americans have seen mariachi bands in films, on TV, and entertaining in Mexican restaurants.

Mariachi music has elements in common with some other forms of Mexican music: the love of song and dance forms such as the **ballad**, **polka**, and **waltz** brought over by

**Above: A mariachi band—with violins, a large *guitarrón,* and Spanish guitars— performs in a park in Mexico City.**

Right: The Mexican hero Francisco "Pancho" Villa, seen here in 1911 leading the rebels during the Mexican Revolution. He has inspired the lyrics of many Mexican ballads.

Europeans who occupied Mexico at various times, and of the instruments used in those forms, such as the violin and trumpet, the Spanish guitar and its larger, lower-**toned** Mexican cousin, the *guitarrón*.

The name "mariachi" is said to have come from the French word for marriage. Mariachi bands began among the peasants hired to play at weddings and society events at the beginning of the 20th century. These peasants, from the western Mexican state of Jalisco, used to adopt the fancy dress of their wealthier employers. That is how the mariachi fashion of tightly tailored pants and jackets with brass buttons first began.

### Songs from the Revolution

When the Mexican Revolution against the aristocratic government backed by the U.S. began in 1910, the rebelling peasants told stories of their heroes—including the bandit Francisco "Pancho" Villa—in ballads called *corridos*. This song form, written in waltz or **march** time, often featured two or three singers accompanied by guitar or accordion. The **lyrics** of the first *corridos* were about the struggles for territory between the U.S. and Mexico. The *corridos* of today, however, deal with such topical matters as the earthquake in the San Francisco Bay area in 1989 or the adventures of drug smugglers.

### On the borderline

The story form and waltz and march **rhythms** of *corrido* were combined with polka to make a music that was widely popular on both sides of the border between the U.S. and Mexico. This music was called *norteño* on the Mexican side and Tex-Mex on the U.S. side. A version of this music that concentrates on the danceable polka beat rather than the nasal vocal style of *norteño* is called *conjunto*, which is also the name for the kind of groups that play it. Its lyrics deal with the struggles for love and money. In the 1930s the skill of players like Don Santiago Jimenez (1919–1984) and his son (b. 1939)—nicknamed "Flaco," which means "Skinny"—helped make the accordion a favorite instrument in this

**Above: The Mexican Flaco Jimenez's masterful accordion playing has helped make this instrument a vital ingredient of *conjunto* music.**

**Below: The group Los Lobos mixes *norteño* and rock to create a more modern music.**

style of music. In the 1950s the accordion player Tony De La Rosa (b. 1931) added bass and drums to "anchor" the danceable beat, and by the 1960s he had become the most popular performer of *conjunto*.

Later, a very successful *norteño* group called Los Tigres del Norte added brass instruments to *norteño* to create a style called *banda*. This music is played by *bandas*—groups of between four and 20 musicians who play brass and percussion instruments, with an occasional guitar thrown in. *Banda* has become the most popular music in Mexico today, dominating TV music programs and concert venues—except in Mexico City, where *cumbia* and salsa are more popular.

Other groups have become successful by adding rock to the *norteño* style. The most famous of these is Los Lobos. Although they come from California, they have stuck firmly to the Mexican *norteño* form, which can be heard in their extremely successful version of "La Bamba," released in 1988.

### Back at the ranch

Ranchera, as the name suggests, is the Mexican match for U.S. country and western music. Its highly emotional singing is meant to be listened to, not necessarily danced to, and its lyrics are about living in the city and longing for country life. The singing style is characterized by the way the singer holds out the last note of the last word of a lyric and adds a glissando— when one note slides into the next note. Rock singer Linda Ronstadt (b. 1946), whose father was a Mexican immigrant, helped spread her musical inheritance with a 1987 album of ranchera she recorded with Daniel Valdez and the Mariachi Vargas band.

### The brother of *son*

*Huapango* is a regional style from central and eastern Mexico that is similar to Cuban *son* (see page 8). The style is little known in the U.S. except in the highly changed form of the song "La Bamba," which was turned into a rock hit in 1958 by the U.S.-Mexican singer and guitarist Ritchie Valens (1941–1959). There are several types of *huapango*: the *huasteco*, which has **improvised** lyrics sung in falsetto (an artificially high

Left: Ritchie Valens, who died in the same 1959 plane crash as the famous rock singer Buddy Holly, had a huge hit the year before with a much-altered version of a *huapango* song called "La Bamba."

Below: This Inca pottery found in Peru shows a man playing an ancient flute.

later by Europeans. Wind and percussion instruments from the ruins around Lake Titicaca, on the border between modern-day Bolivia and Peru, are thought to date back to 10,000 B.C.—before the pyramids of Egypt were built. When the Inca Empire took over these two countries, along with Ecuador, in about 1200 B.C., the new rulers apparently allowed the conquered peoples to keep their languages, musics, and religions, which were rooted in their calendar and in the natural forces that influenced their agricultural activities.

The Spanish conquistadors who arrived in the region in the 16th century overthrew the Inca and introduced the Catholic religion and Spanish melodies and instruments. Yet the ancient Andeans (sometimes called "Indians") continued to play and sing their own kinds of songs in their own languages, accompanied by their own instruments. The Andeans still play their own music and instruments today—even those who have left the isolated mountain villages to live in large cities near or on the coast of the Pacific Ocean.

voice), accompanied by guitars; the *arribeño*, which uses an old form of Spanish musical poetry called *décimas* (see page 11); and the *veracruzano*, which is most often accompanied by the lush sound of a harp.

Mexico has borrowed many musical styles from its neighbors to the east and south, especially salsa from Cuba and *cumbia* from Colombia. *Cumbia*, partly because of its danceability, has at times been more popular in Mexico than any other kind of music and even more popular there than in its native Colombia.

## Ancient Andean music

The music made by the people of the high Andes Mountains in South America is among the oldest on earth and has survived the invasions by the Inca and

## Instruments of the Andes

The instruments used in Andean music are among the most ancient and interesting in the world. The panpipe—a set of 13 or more wooden or clay whistles bound together to create a range of tones—is similar to the ancient Greek instrument of the same name (see Volume 1, pages 7 and 9). The Andean version comes in different regional types but bears the collective name of *siku*. The smaller Peruvian version is called the *antara* and is played by one person. It plays the five notes (D, E, F-**sharp**, A, and B) that

**Pentatonic Scale**

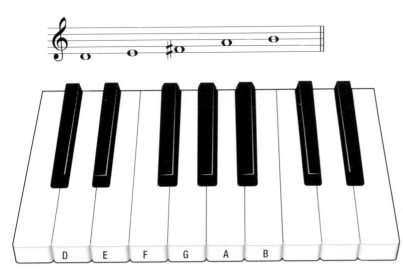

**Above:** Dating from about 2000 B.C., the pentatonic scale is one of the oldest known scales. It is made up of five notes (*pente* means "five" in Greek) and can be heard by playing the notes D, E, F-sharp, A, and B on the keyboard. The scale is used in many countries worldwide; the Scottish song "Auld Lang Syne" is an example of a song in the Western world that is based on the pentatonic scale.

make up the traditional pentatonic (five-tone) **scale** heard throughout Andean music.

The Ecuadorian *rondador* is also played by one person, but two of its pipes can be played at once, which allows **harmonies** to be created. For the more popular panpipe called *zampoña* and the much larger *toyos*—which can extend up to 54 inches in length—the melodies of the music are divided between two players.

**Right:** Two Andean panpipes of different sizes are often played together by one musician.

Another instrument of the region is the *kena*—a hollow tube a little over 14 inches long, with holes along the tube and a notch at the blown end. The oldest *kenas*, dating back some 5,000 years, were made from animal or human bones. However, more recent *kenas* are made from clay, wood, or plastic. The instrument originally played a pentatonic scale and was used by shepherds to scare away wolves; but even after the conquering Spanish introduced the 12-tone scale, pentatonic melodies were preferred.

Today, community groups in the Andes play square Bolivian flutes called *tarkas*, which are tuned in **intervals** a fifth apart from each other—such as C and G, A and E. This results in the creation of intense, compelling harmonies and produces an open, misty sound. Some of these Andean wind instruments were originally accompanied by drums formed from sections of tree trunk covered by leather or animal skin, and

Left: These long panpipes, made from paper, are being played by musicians in a procession outside the Church of San Ignacio de Moxos in El Beni, Bolivia, in celebration of Saint Ignacio's feast day.

by rattles made from goats' hooves sewn onto a piece of fabric. The Bolivians also came up with the *charango*, their own ten-stringed cousin of the guitar and mandolin. The body of the *charango* was originally made from the round, hard shell of an animal called the armadillo. Instruments such as the violin and saxophone are also played in the Andes in a manner similar to that in the U.S. and Europe, although sometimes in different **tunings**. A harp is also sometimes used, but in festival processions it is hung over the shoulder and played backhanded, quite differently from in a classical orchestra, where the player is seated with the harp in front.

## Andean music forms

Below: *Cantu*—one of the oldest styles of music still played in the Andean region— is performed on drums and reed panpipes in a parade to mark a farmers' festival in Bolivia.

Probably the oldest Andean music form still played is the *cantu*. It is performed in villages during festivals with only percussion and traditional wind instruments. The musical form most familiar outside the Andes may well be *huayno* (pronounced "why- no"). This is perhaps because the U.S.

folk-pop singers Simon and Garfunkel put English lyrics to one pentatonic *huayno*, "El Condor Pasa," in 1970. The song was composed in the 18th century when the last descendant of the Incan emperors died.

Aside from the pentatonic scale and some of the instruments, Andean songs also differ from U.S. and European songs in the way they are sung—in high, piercing voices. The **modulation** of many *huaynos* from **minor** to **major modes** and back again gives them what sounds like a sad-yet-happy mood.

Andean tradition is at its strongest in Bolivia, which has no sea coast. In Peru and Ecuador there has been more of a mixing of *huaynos* and other forms with the music of Afro-Caribbean and European peoples, particularly in the cities. Some of the results of this musical mix are called *marinera*—which is danced to by people from the richer neighborhoods of Lima in Peru—and *muliza*, which is played on harp, fiddle, saxophone, and clarinet to accompany various types of European dances.

# THE SOUND OF CHICHA

Left: The *chicha* band Belen use a combination of rock and traditional Andean instruments in their music.

In the 1960s a music form called *chicha* was created that mixed *cumbia* (see page 23) and *huayno* (see page 25) with rock 'n' roll. The first *chicha* hit was written by the band Los Demonios de Mantaro ("The Demons of Mantaro") and was called *"La Chichera"* ("The Chicha Seller")—a favorite Andean drink that became the name for this type of music. Some of the best known *chicha* groups are Los Shapis, who became famous with their hit song *"El aguajal"* ("The Swamp") in 1981, and Belen. By the mid-1980s *chicha* had become the most widespread music in the cities of Peru. The instruments used in *chicha* include guitars, electric bass, electric organ, timbales, congas, and sometimes a synthesizer. The bands have one or more singers, who may also play percussion, and their lyrics are about the sufferings of Peruvian people in love and in society. The sounds of the Andes have been borrowed by other politically minded groups writing new songs, called *nuevo canción* in Spanish (see page 30), about the hardships of Andean people and their neighbors in northern Chile.

CHICHA
BELEN
the drink... the culture... the music
Chicha

**Right: Belen is the first *chicha* band to have an album released in the West.**

### The powerful Brazilian mix

Despite its great distance from Europe and the U.S., and the uniqueness of its language (Portuguese), Brazil has had a powerful and exciting influence on a variety of musical forms in other parts of the world, including jazz and rock. This is due in part to its history—the arrival of the Portuguese explorer Cabral in Brazil in 1500 was the beginning of a more complete mix

of peoples and cultures than had occurred in most other countries.

Many of the native Amerindians who survived the hard labor and disease brought by the arrival of the Europeans were exiled to the far reaches of the Amazon rainforest in what is the northwest of present-day Brazil. Some of them were taught Catholic church music and "civilized" habits by the Jesuit priests who came to set up missions, although the native people had their own music and instruments. This meeting of cultures, and some of the resulting music, is shown in a 1986 movie

---

## Brazilian music has had an exciting influence on both jazz and rock

---

called *The Mission*. Traces of Brazilian music before European influence can still be found in the rainforest.

As in the Caribbean and elsewhere in the Americas, the conquering Europeans had slaves sent from West and Central Africa, believing that this area could provide them with more and often stronger slaves than could be found among the Amerindians. The Africans brought their own kinds of drums and other instruments with them, as well as their **syncopated** rhythms, dances, and chants.

More than most other European settlers—especially the Protestant North Americans—the white Portuguese intermarried with the Africans (and, to a lesser degree, with the Indians). This of course mixed the races and helped merge their musics. Several seemingly sad Portuguese ballad forms took on new syncopation in Brazil. One of them was the Portuguese fado that resulted in what

the Portuguese, such as the flute, the clarinet, the guitar, and its smaller cousin the *cavaquinho* (pronounced "ka-va-keen-yo").

## Music on the move

As more and more of Brazil was settled, unique musics developed in each region. In the 20th century ease of travel and the arrival of radio and TV meant that these musics could be shared around the country—and ultimately around the world. The movie *Black Orpheus,* released in 1959, introduced samba to much of the world by filming the Lenten festival, called *Carnaval,* in the city of Rio. The movie shows scenes of a joyous, noisy parade, featuring floats and amplified samba songs with lyrics about historical, political, or fantasy themes and throngs of happy dancers, many of them wearing wild costumes or very little at all. *Carnaval* parades had been happening 40 years before the filming of *Black Orpheus* and still continue today in the Brazilian cities of Rio de Janeiro, Salvador, São Paulo, and elsewhere.

is known today as *choro* (pronounced "show-ho," and which may have taken its name from the Portuguese word for weeping or sobbing). *Choro* is a quiet instrumental music that mixes European waltz and polka rhythms with African syncopation. The band Os Ingênuos ("Simply for you"), from Salvador de Bahia in Brazil, is one of the best examples of a *choro* group still recording today.

Another kind of music that mixes a sad-sounding Portuguese form and a syncopated rhythm is *pagode* ("pa-go-jee"). With lyrics about love and Brazilian history, this music, often played without drums, developed in bars and cafés. It is related to the more famous—and much livelier and noisier—**samba**, considered to be *choro*'s opposite.

A mixture also occurred between African instruments, such as the *agogo* (double cowbell) and the *cuica* (a drum that sounds like birds or monkey and human chatter when rubbed), and European instruments like the triangle and a large tambourine called the *pandeiro.* These instruments added exciting sound textures when they accompanied instruments popular with

**Above: The movie *The Mission* featured Amerindian music from the rainforest.**

**Below: The band Os Ingênuos uses *choro* instruments like the *cavaquinho* (bottom left) and the *pandeiro* (bottom right).**

The rhythm of samba music is based on a relaxed 2/4 beat (counted as 1-2, 1-2) overlaid with powerful syncopated rhythms. There are many forms of samba. The loud and flashy samba used in the samba-school street parades—with its call-and-response vocals accompanied by masses of drummers—is known as *samba de enredo*. A slowed-down version of samba is called *samba-cançao* ("song samba"). This type of samba is found in clubs and dancehalls, performed by a singer and a band centered around guitar and percussion. Offshoot forms of *samba-cançao* include *samba breque* ("break samba"), with a choppy reggaelike rhythm, and the more recent *samba do pagode* (see page 27). It was this quiet *pagode* style, played by such bands as Raa Negra, that introduced Brazilian music to rock star David Byrne and resulted in the formation of his Luaka Bop record

label to release Brazilian music albums. Other performers who have recorded *pagodes* are Agepê (1942–1995), Clara Nunes (1943–1989), and Alcione (b. 1947).

**Making way for the bossa**

In the late 1950s musicians were also turning samba, *choro*, and other forms into a quieter, jazz-influenced music called bossa nova, which loosely means "new style." Its chief creators, especially Antonio Carlos Jobim (1927–1994), have received attention outside Brazil, partly because their music appeared in the movie *Black Orpheus* and partly because U.S. jazz players had started to record their songs, most notably saxophonist Stan Getz (b. 1927). "The Girl from Ipanema"—a dreamy song written by Jobim and recorded by Getz and Brazilians João Gilberto (b. 1931) and his then-wife Astrud

# CARNIVAL TIME

Brazil is famous for its *Carnaval*. Although many other Catholic countries have carnivals to celebrate the arrival of Lent on the Christian calendar, none do it with quite the same style and enthusiasm as Brazil. The entire country shuts down for five days, and everybody joins the party. There are huge parades, decorative floats, colorful costumes, and wild dancing. But the most important element of the Brazilian *Carnaval* is the samba music. New songs are specially written for the *Carnaval,* and songwriters and musicians enter into a swirl of competition—fueled by TV and radio programs—to create the greatest *Carnaval* hit of the year.

The *Carnaval* in Rio de Janeiro is the most famous, with people flocking to the city from far and wide to see its parade of the samba schools—an overpowering show of thundering, body-tingling drum rhythms. Two other large Brazilian *Carnavals* take place in Salvador and Olinda, and unlike the Rio *Carnaval*, with its rows of spectators, everyone gets out on the street and dances to the music of bands that perform on large trucks loaded with sound systems. The musical bonanza of *Carnaval* breathes fresh life into samba every year, making sure this music continues to develop, and bringing it to the ears of more and more international visitors.

**Left: A samba parade marches down the street at the Rio *Carnaval*.**

equator listened on shortwave radio to Caribbean music, including **calypso** from Trinidad and **reggae** from Jamaica, and to the music of neighboring Latin American countries. From this mix they created a sexy dance called the **lambada**.

Many Brazilian regional song forms were popularized in televised festivals held in the late 1960s and 1970s. The lyrics of the songs, many of them composed by college students, often complained about the military dictatorship then controlling Brazil. This younger generation's music became known as MPB ("*musica popular brasileira*" in Portuguese). Some of the songwriters—including such future stars as Caetano Veloso (b. 1942), Gilberto Gil (b. 1942), Gal Costa (b. 1945), and Milton Nascimento (b. 1942)—began using electric guitar and bass alongside traditional instruments. This movement, know as Tropicalismo,

(b. 1940)—became a big hit in 1962. It crossed from the sophisticated clubs of Rio and São Paulo to the U.S., and then from jazz to rock radio stations. Everyone seemed to love its gentle syncopation, swaying melody, and lyrics (translated from Portuguese into English) about a guy who longs for a beautiful girl as she passes by.

## Brazil's regional songs

In the state of Bahia, farther to the north, traditional music had been closer to the rhythms and drumming sounds of Africa. As in Cuba, music was part of the celebration of the ancient African gods who were matched with Catholic saints.

The dry, poor, and mostly white northeastern region of the country gave rise to *forro*, a fast, chattering song form accompanied by the accordion. People living farther to the northwest and closer to the

**Below: Gilberto Gil, one of the founders of Tropicalismo, faced fierce criticism for his "unpatriotic" music.**

was controversial and was rejected by the press and the government as unpatriotic. However, attitudes changed and the stars of Tropicalismo, and even some of the older bossa nova artists and their younger imitators, are still recording and performing around the world. Brazilians, in turn, especially in the cities, are very much interested in the latest U.S. pop music and have formed plenty of their own bands to play **grunge**, **heavy metal**, and **rap**.

## Chilean music

Relatively little of Chile's music has traveled outside the country, except for *nueva canción*—the "new song" movement (see page 18) that helped lift the spirits of Chileans under the dictatorship of General Augusto Pinochet in the 1960s. Yet some of the melodies of *nueva canción* and other Chilean folk forms can be traced back to the music brought to South America by the Spanish conquistadors in the early 16th century. These forms include the *verso*, a ritual country folksong based on poems from the Spanish court; the *canto a lo pueta*, meaning "singing in the style of the poet," which functions as a song contest between men; and the *tonada* (tune), sung by women in the central Chilean countryside, accompanied by guitar or accordion.

Some aspects of the pre-European Amerindians—among them the Incas from northern Chile and the Araucanians from the center—have survived, and their music has often blended with other influences. Their sound can be heard in saints' festivals in central Chile, where players on one-note vertical flutes perform in *hocket*, in which a single melody passes among the players who play or sing the different notes in alternation, accompanied by drums. Dancers in

the north move to Andean rhythms and melodies played on panpipes, fifes, and drums. Some *nuevo canción* groups have used Andean sounds, the most famous of which is the Chilean group Inti Illimani.

The guitar, widely popular throughout the continent, is played in several different styles in various regions of Chile. Other stringed instruments include the *bandutría*, with a pear-shaped body and six pairs of double strings, and the *bandola*, teardrop-shaped with four sets of double strings, as well as two sets of triple strings. All of these instruments are found in the central part of the country. Chile shares the harp and the *zampoña* (panpipes) with the Andean countries to the north (see page 24).

## Argentinian tango

Argentina, the big country across the Andes from Chile, is one of the few to have gained worldwide attention

Above: One of the great stars of Chilean *nueva canción* was Victor Jara. After studying for the priesthood, he became a soldier, and then an actor and theater director, before turning his lyrical voice, love of Chilean folk music, and concern for his fellow man to writing political songs. For this he was murdered by Chile's right-wing military in 1973.

Left: The Argentinian tango—with its slow and sexy syncopated rhythm in 2/4 time— swept the dancehalls of the world in the 1920s and 1930s and became one of the most popular ballroom dances of the 20th century.

for a single musical form—the tango, a stylish dance of love, with a serious, insistent rhythm. It was played at first on guitar, violin, and flute and later led by a large accordion called a *bandoneón*. It moved in popularity from the working-class night spots of Buenos Aires, Argentina's largest city, to the nation's wealthier communities and onto dance floors across the world in the 1920s and 1930s.

Hollywood ultimately put the glamorous and "outrageous" image of tango onto the big screen, but the music gained more respect through the composition and performing talent of *bandoneón* master Astor Piazzolla (1921–1992). He added jazz and classical music sounds to the tango in the 1960s and called it *nuevo tango* ("new tango").

## Other forms of music

One of the biggest international stars from Argentina, aside from Piazzolla, is Mercedes Sosa (b. 1935)—the dramatic singer of a very different music, which also appeared in Cuba and Chile. She helped coin the term "*neuva canción*" in 1962, a good seven years before neighboring Chile held its first "new song" festival. Sixteen years later she was expelled from her country during its own period of military dictatorship, but not before she and like-minded Argentinians had helped repopularize several folk-song forms, including the *chacarera*, *zamba*, and *chamame*. The rhythms of *chacarera* and *zamba* are similar, only the *chacarera* is faster, and the *zamba* has more of a skip in its beat. A singer, guitar, and an Argentinian drum called the *bombo*—made from a hollowed tree trunk covered by animal skins at both ends—are used in both forms. *Chamame* is a combination of the polka, waltz, and a popular Polish

dance called the **mazurka**, and is accompanied by the *bandoneón* and the button accordion. It is danced by a larger number of Argentinians today than the more international tango.

These music forms and those of Uruguay (the capital of which, Montevideo, lies close to Buenos Aires across the Rio de la Plata) show far fewer influences of Amerindian or African cultures than do most other parts of South America, mainly because there are fewer such people living there. However, Argentina and Uruguay share the *copla* (couplet), a Spanish poetic form set to music, and the *milónga*—a song form with possible connections to romantic ballads from the early colonial era. So although Argentina is more likely to bring to mind tightly embraced couples dancing the tango, the gauchos—who once tended cattle on Argentina's interior pampas (grasslands)—have their own music. They stomped their boots to the sound of *milónga* long before the tango took hold. These traditional forms of music still remain in Latin America, despite the creation of more modern music forms.

**Above: Argentinian singer Mercedes Sosa inspires much passion with her deep, warm, and haunting voice as she sings about such sensitive subjects as love, poverty, and politics. Her political stance caused her performances to be banned in her own country and forced her into exile until the collapse of Argentina's military government in 1982.**

# CHAPTER 3

# The Caribbean

The music of the Caribbean is a rich, complex musical stew: a result of the history and geography of the area that has mixed many different peoples and influences together.

Mixing of musics occurs wherever history and geography bring different peoples together. As time goes on, it becomes harder to separate the ingredients, and the music of the Caribbean is a good example of the type of rich, complex musical stew that can emerge from such conditions. Over the centuries the small island territories and countries spread across that warm, beautiful sea have been influenced by the Amerindians, who first settled the islands, then by a variety of Europeans with their many different languages and musics. The African slaves that the Europeans brought to the islands also added their musical traditions to

**Above: Carnival in Trinidad, held annually in March, features thunderous calypso played by steel bands that have come to symbolize the music of the Caribbean.**

this rich stew. Finally these countries were influenced by each other and by the nearby countries of the U.S. and South America. That the Caribbean islands are so small and close together made the mixing easier, and the process has sped up in the 20th century, thanks to recordings, radio, TV, and tourism.

The effect of all this transportation of musical traditions can be seen on the island nation of Cuba, with its combination of Spanish and African culture, and then its effect in turn on the U.S. and the rest of the world, particularly through salsa (see Chapter 1). This chapter covers the rest of the Caribbean, starting out with a look at how these islands developed.

## Colonial influence

The island of Hispaniola ("Little Spain"), to the east of Cuba, was split between two European languages when the Spanish gave part of it to France in 1697. French-speaking Haiti was created to the west, while what later became known as the Dominican Republic was set up on the Spanish-speaking eastern two-thirds of the island. Puerto Rico, east of Hispaniola, was claimed as a U.S. territory after the American victory in the Spanish-American War of 1898.

The group of islands called the Lesser Antilles, southeast of Puerto Rico, were mostly French. But the British claimed several of the smaller islands, as well as Jamaica, to the south of Cuba, and the Bahamas, to the north near Florida. Off the coast of South America, far to the south, Britain also colonized Barbados and later took Grenada and Tobago from France and Trinidad from Spain. Most of the larger Caribbean islands are now independent countries, despite retaining the languages and other aspects of colonial culture.

## Flavors of merengue

Due to the fact that the islands are so close together, it is not surprising to find that the **merengue** music of the Dominican Republic and the *méringue* of neighboring Haiti sound similar. But the Dominican form is quicker, and there is no mistaking the crisp, **syncopated** beat of the music, in 2/4 time. It is performed by several vocalists in Spanish, often to the accompaniment of a large accordion, a two-headed drum called the *tambora*, the güiro left behind by the Arawak Indians, and the conga adopted from Central Africa. The Haitian *méringue* features a guitar and **lyrics** sung in a form of French called Creole (often written "Kreyol").

Both musics are based in African **rhythms** and percussion, as is salsa (which they resemble), but the most modern merengue also makes use of the saxophone. Merengue was encouraged by Dominican dictator Rafael Trujillo as a sign of national pride and to improve the popularity

**Above: A religious ceremony on the island of Hispaniola is accompanied by dancers, drummers, and pipers.**

Right: "Dynamaestro" Francisco Ulloa's CD *Ultramerengue* keeps alive the merengue tradition of superfast accordion playing.

SQUEEZEBOX MERENGUE from the DOMINICAN DYNAMAESTRO

FRANCISCO ULLOA
Y SU CONJUNTO TIPICO DOMINICANO
¡ULTRAMERENGUE!

of his rule from the 1930s to 1950s. Merengue continued in the 1960s and 1970s under a more relaxed political regime, with Johnny Ventura mixing the music with rock 'n' roll, and Francisco Ulloa (b. 1954) maintaining the more traditional role of the superfast accordionist. By 2000 the world's biggest merengue star was Juan Luís Guerra (b. 1961). With his group 4:40, he mixed a slowed-down version of merengue with clever vocal **harmonies** to produce some of the hottest Latin music on the scene.

## You can do voodoo

Haiti has not been as successful as its neighbor in moving away from foreign rule toward democracy, even though it had been the first of the Caribbean colonies to become independent and the first black nation anywhere during colonial times. After an unsuccessful slave revolt led by Boukman—a priest of the West African religion called voodoo or *voudou*—another slave named Toussaint L'Ouverture defeated the French colonialists and created Haiti in 1804.

Voodoo, a term referring to both "good" and "bad" spirits, flourished in the new country of Haiti partly because it allowed the worship of Catholic saints (as had the African cultures in Cuba and Brazil). The vocal and drumming patterns of voodoo ceremonies continue to be used today by a few performing and recording groups such as Grupo Mackandal and Rara Machine. Their music matches voodoo with the music of the annual Easter carnival, putting horns and electronic instruments alongside roots rhythms, African drums, and percussion.

Right: The rhythms of a drummer are used to fill this dancer with the spirit of his African ancestors at a voodoo ceremony in Gonaives, Haiti.

## Musical mix

A more recent Haitian development is *compas*. It mixes Haitian *méringue* with the influence of early jazz, which came to the country during the U.S. occupation from 1915 to 1934. It also includes touches of salsa from nearby Cuba and more recently *soca* (see page 41) from the British islands, *soukous* (see pages 62–65) from contemporary Central Africa and *zouk* (see below) from the French Antilles. *Compas* is smoother than the voodoo-related music styles and is performed by large groups resembling jazz bands. The so-called mini-jazz bands of the late 1990s are even closer to U.S., British, and European pop music.

Both the African and more modern forms of music have suffered since the 1960s under the rule of Papa Doc and Baby Doc Duvalier and the military coup that overthrew democratically elected Father Jean-Bertrand Aristide in 1991. U.S. tourism has practically disappeared, and many of the Haitians who fled to the U.S. were musicians, several of whom now perform and record in New York and Miami.

---

## *In contrast to the troubled history of Haiti, its music has always been joyful*

---

In contrast to the troubled history of Haiti, its music has always been joyful, melodic, and good to dance to. There are several young bands, such as Tropicana and Foula, that are still based on the island. But there is also a big Haitian music scene in New York, where bands such as Boukman Eksperyans and Bouka Guinee have been based since they were forced to leave home by a government that branded their music as "too violent."

## Zouk: from Paris to Africa

Music from the French Antilles, south of Hispaniola, has pleased musicians and dancers from Paris to Africa. *Zouk*, the most popular musical form from these islands, is an offshoot of the *gwo ka*, "roots" music (folk music) of the island of Guadeloupe, and *chouval bwa* from Martinique. *Gwo ka* depends on groups of West African-style drummers that travel around the island with tuneful singers during the annual carnival (celebrated before Lent and similar to the carnival in Brazil and the Mardi Gras in New Orleans). *Chouval bwa's* bass drum, the bel-air, is large enough for its player to sit on, while the smaller *tambours* are hung around the neck. Others of the ensemble play bamboo chunks or shakers, with everyone joining in the call-and-response singing (the lead singer calls, and the **chorus** responds, as is done in Central and West Africa).

The European side of *zouk* comes from the older *biguine*, begun by people from Martinique who had seen

Left: Dédé St. Prix carries on a great *zouk* tradition of flute playing. His music updates traditional Martiniquan tunes using a wide range of dance rhythms.

and heard music outside their island while serving as soldiers in World War I. After returning home, they incorporated stringed instruments, woodwind, and horns into the island sound. The result, the *biguine*, became a minor dance craze in Europe and the U.S. when it was adopted by jazz bands in those parts of the world. Back in the Caribbean, *biguine* spun off into a new music called cadence, which was popularized by Haitian orchestras.

In the latter part of the 20th century *zouk* was born, absorbing other Caribbean rhythms and instruments as well as the bright horn **arrangements** of jazz and the electrified excitement of rock 'n' roll. *Zouk* then took off across the water, influencing African music and Brazil's *lambada*. During the 1980s, at the height of *zouk*'s popularity, bands like Kassav and Zouk Machine led the way. Since then it has become less popular outside the Caribbean, but the music is still enormously popular locally.

## Roots, rock, reggae

The Caribbean music that has been most popular internationally, aside from salsa, has been **reggae** from Jamaica. Since the 1970s its throbbing rhythm has been a major form of music in the U.S., Britain, and Africa, as well as at home. Reggae's strength has come from its roots in black history, spiritualism, and politics. It has grown through the many opportunities in Jamaica to record and be heard live and over massive sound systems.

The roots of reggae date back to black slaves of the Spanish colonizers. The slaves fled to the hills when the British seized control of Jamaica in the late 17th century. Later, after the abolition of slavery West Africans brought over to work on the new

plantations developed their own folk music, with elements borrowed from Spanish, British, and Christian religious music as well as from their own traditions. The church was popular in Jamaica in the 19th century, when a great religious revival swept the island, and music played a great part in its regular rituals.

During the 20th century the Rastafari faith became popular, which believes in a return to Africa, universal peace, and the spiritual use of marijuana, all of which have found their way into the lyrics of reggae.

Before reggae, though, the most popular song form was *mento*, with its breezy **tempo** and naughty lyrics. Then, after World War II Jamaicans began buying radios, **phonographs**, and the kind of U.S. music that came to be called **rhythm and blues** and later gave way to early rock 'n' roll. The Jamaicans became fond of sound systems, their term for large speakers that could be set up on the beach, in dancehalls, and elsewhere to play their favorite music very loudly. This encouraged the production of records by their own musicians and the

**Below: In Jamaica sound systems continue to be the people's favorite way of listening to music.**

**Left: Lee Perry is responsible for some of the most vital music to have come from Jamaica.**

reggae, appearing in the late 1960s and early 1970s, made a popular, danceable mix of rock steady's beat and *mento*'s skittering melodies, giving Rastafarian songwriters a means of spreading their messages. A key player in the development of reggae was Lee "Scratch" Perry (b. 1936). A fine vocalist and an innovative producer, his Black Ark studio was the venue for some of the most popular reggae recordings of the time.

### The Harder They Come

Just as **samba** had been introduced to many Americans through the soundtrack to the 1959 Brazilian-French movie *Black Orpheus*, Americans began to discover reggae via the 1973 Jamaican film *The Harder They Come* and its singing star, Jimmy Cliff (b. 1948).

At about the same time reggae acts began touring the world. Among them were Toots and the Maytals, who appeared on the soundtrack for *The Harder They Come*, and the Wailers, which included three future

development of special ways of presenting the music, including having disc jockeys (DJs) talking over the records while they played.

U.S. rhythm and blues turned into **ska** in Jamaican recordings. In ska the usual rhythm and blues **backbeat**—the percussive beat of the tune—was misheard or misplayed, usually resulting in more beats. This created music that sounded offbeat and often manic in its rhythm, a new kind of music that had some of the brassy high spirits of jazz.

Jamaica became independent of the British Empire in 1962, but poverty and political corruption plagued the new nation, and ska was followed by the slow, bass-heavy sound of **rock steady**, with lyrics about the island's problems. Then

**Below: A poster for the reggae movie *The Harder They Come*.**

# BOB MARLEY

Perhaps the most famous reggae performer of all time is the late Bob Marley. His recordings with his band the Wailers have sold millions of copies in the U.S., in Europe, and in Africa, particularly the albums *Catch a Fire*, *Burnin'* (both 1973), and *Live at the Lyceum* (1975). His music dealt with social and political issues, and for a time in the mid-1970s Marley became a symbol of rebellion all over the world. But his songs also have topics that everyone understands—spirituality, life, love, and loss—and this made his appeal more widespread than many other more religious reggae artists. His status and influence as a "rock" star were most prominent when he organized a concert on the eve of the Jamaican election in 1978. During his performance he invited the opposing leaders, Michael Manley and Edward Seaga, to appear on stage with him. In an effort to stop the violence that had marked the election campaign, he symbolically linked the arms of the two leaders while singing "One Love," a song about peace and brotherhood. Marley died of cancer in 1981.

**Above: Singer-songwriter and guitarist Bob Marley is photographed in full swing at a performance in 1975.**

superstars: Peter Tosh (1944–1987), Bunny Wailer (b. 1947), and Bob Marley (1945–1981).

Although Jimmy Cliff and Marley placed great importance on political and spiritual messages, other reggae artists concentrated on changing the sound of the music, sometimes by electronically removing vocals and adding echo and other strange effects to create what's known as **dub**. Artists such as King Tubby (1941–1989) and Augustus Pablo (b. *c.*1954) were important in shaping this music. By the late 1970s and early 1980s DJs like U-Roy (b. 1942) and Big Youth (b. 1955) had perfected their talkover technique, which was called toasting and became an inspiration for U.S. **rap**. The style of later DJs, such as Buju Banton (b. 1973) and Shabba Ranks (b. 1965), close to **gangsta rap** in terms of tough

**Below: Lucky Dube became the biggest-selling African artist of all time with his "classic" reggae sound of the 1970s.**

and sometimes dirty language, is known as *ragga*, short for ragamuffin, and talks about the dangers of living in the poorer neighborhoods of Jamaica's largest city, Kingston.

Interestingly, South Africa's Lucky Dube (b. 1967), pronounced "Du-bay"—the biggest-selling African artist of all time—performs a reggae much closer to the "classic" sound and lyrics of Marley, Wailer, and Tosh. Reggae also has performers in West Africa, Poland, Japan, Brazil, and Britain.

### Rhyming spirituals

The Bahamas, another former British colony to the north of Cuba, hasn't provided anything as musically important as reggae. However, one of its musicians, Joseph Spence (1910–1984), is admired by many **world music** fans and pop artists, among them Ry Cooder (b. 1947),

Taj Mahal (b. 1942), and the Grateful Dead. Spence continued a tradition dating back some 200 years to when British Loyalists had abandoned their plantations in the Carolinas during the American Revolution. These Britons came to the Bahamas, bringing their black slaves, who had their own versions of **hymns** they had learned in the Protestant churches their owners had forced them to attend.

The Bahamian blacks were joined in the middle of the next century by runaway slaves from North America. The black population remained economically and socially segregated from Bahama's whites, but they kept their love of old Christian hymns. They performed them, though, in the exciting call-and-response style that had come over from West and Central Africa. In these "rhyming spirituals" a phrase from the Gospel is repeated by a chorus of men and women, while a soloist, often a high **tenor** or a woman, **improvises** rhythmically, melodically, and quite wildly.

## Harmonies on guitar

Spence was recorded by visiting Americans such as Alan Lomax, Sam Charters, Jody Stecher, and Peter Siegel, with or without the vocal support of his wife, relatives, and friends, and with or without his amazing guitar playing. His magic was that he was able to play all the different parts of a song's harmony at the same time. He brought a similar approach to sea chanteys and even to reworkings of U.S. popular songs.

Unfortunately, there has been very little interest from tourists in this fascinating island music since Spence's death and Bahamas's independence in 1973. Yet young Bahamian bands continue to record their own, more commercial music, based partly in U.S. rock, partly in *soca* borrowed

from Trinidad and Tobago, and partly in the tricky *goombay* music of Junkanoo, the annual Christmastime pageant that takes over the streets of downtown Nassau, the nation's capital. Traditional forms such as rake-and-scrape (named for the musical saw that is part of the band) and children's ring games continue both in Nassau and on the country's more remote Out Islands.

## Calypso music

At the opposite end of the Caribbean, near South America, the islands of Trinidad and Tobago had generated a popular song form, **calypso**, long before they gained joint independence from Britain in 1962. Calypso was enjoyed in the U.S. and England

**Above: A Junkanoo Parade costume in the streets of Nassau, the capital city of the Bahamas.**

THE STORY OF MUSIC

partly because of its lyrics about current affairs and romance, sung in an odd style of English called pidgin. But the form dates back to the French settlers who took control of Trinidad from the Spanish in the late 18th century, and who arrived with their slaves from Haiti and the French

Antilles. Some of the French "patois" language can still be found on the islands and in songs.

When West Africans came to the plantations of Tobago and Trinidad, they brought with them a form of work song called *gayup*, featuring a lead singer called a chantwell. In the 19th century chantwells competed during the pre-Lenten carnival for the title of "King" and were accompanied by bands of drums and bamboo tubes. Early in the next century, when the music was named calypso, instruments from traditional jazz bands were added. The song lyrics sometimes protested about the difficult conditions of island blacks in amusing ways and also poked fun at rival chantwells and their bands.

With the invention of the popular steel bands in the 1950s—bands of musicians who all played steel drums—local music developed rapidly, and steel bands began to replace the older bamboo and jazz bands. As a music to party to, especially at

## THE STEEL DRUM

When the U.S. set up naval bases on the island of Trinidad during World War II, they took with them a huge number of oil drums, the contents of which fueled their ships. When the drums were empty, they were used to create a new percussion instrument. The lids of the drums were shaped with hammers to create the **tones** of a musical **scale**, and they are played with rubber-tipped sticks. The steel "pan" is one of the few acoustic instruments to have been invented in the 20th century. The early steel bands in Port of Spain, the capital of Trinidad, earned a certain reputation through street fighting between rival musicians. In more recent years, however, the steel band movement has been officially recognized, and today bands are often sponsored by local businesses.

Steel bands can feature up to 300 pans, which produce a high-octane sound of enormous energy—a fitting symbol for Trinidad and the carnival.

**Above: The steel pan is the most important acoustic instrument to have been invented in the 20th century.**

---

### *As a music to party to, calypso dominated the Caribbean until the 1970s*

---

carnival, calypso became so popular locally and internationally that it became the dominant sound of the Caribbean until the 1970s, when reggae and salsa took over.

Calypso's main outlet was the carnival; and as the carnival developed, it became more popular and its competitions for Calypso Monarch (best calypso) and Road March (most played calypso) more important. Some calypsonians, such as the Mighty Sparrow (b. 1936), held the title of "King of the Carnival" for

New York rather than Trinidad. Gradually, soul and calypso were combined to name a new form, *soca*, which spread throughout the Caribbean, rivaling salsa, reggae, and calypso in its popularity with both locals and tourists.

*Soca*, very much a dance form, was produced with a wider international audience in mind, and the lyrics tend to avoid social issues and concentrate more on enjoyment. Its greatest moment, perhaps, was the song "Hot, Hot, Hot," recorded by the group Arrow in 1984. The song became so successful that many people associate it with Caribbean-style festivals held all over the world.

However, along with success has come complaints from traditionalists that *soca* has destroyed the old calypso. Once the emphasis of the music was on politics, and songs featured lyrics that were intended to convey the feelings of the people; now the emphasis is on dance and attempts to help people forget their troubles and enjoy themselves. In the search for a new audience it could be said that the music has been watered down and lost some of its passion.

several years, but the best-known voice (and image) of calypso outside the Caribbean was Harry Belafonte (b. 1927), a New York actor and singer who had spent his childhood in his parents' homeland of Jamaica. Many of Belafonte's calypso hits on U.S. radio in the 1950s, including "The Banana Boat Song (Day-O)," were actually written by another non-Trinidadian, Irving Burgie (b. 1924) of Barbados. Calypso became so popular that it is now demanded by tourists no matter which part of the Caribbean they are visiting.

## Soul + calypso = *soca*

In the 1970s and 1980s musicians such as the Mighty Sparrow (who was spending part of each year in New York), David Rudder (b. 1953), and other Caribbean artists began updating their music with faster beats borrowed from American **disco** and soul. They also took to recording in

**Below: David Rudder has attempted to continue the tradition of calypso while adding new ideas from outside the island of Trinidad.**

# CHAPTER 4

# India and Its Neighbors

There is a huge output of both traditional and popular music from the Indian subcontinent. Its enormous musical variety is a reflection of the vastness of this region. Although many of the old traditions continue, the late 20th century saw the flowering of exciting new strands of Asian music, such as the bhangra beat of Britain.

Above: Both music and dance are regarded as an important part of the cultural scene in India.

Only in the last half of the 20th century did the U.S. and Europe learn about a classical music that developed much earlier than their own. Although Indian classical music follows strict rules and is at least as difficult to learn to play as Western classical music, it is usually included in the category of **world music** because its exotic sounds have only recently become available to Western ears.

The Indian subcontinent is vast, and the variety of its music is a reflection of that vastness. An important aspect of Indian music is that while Western music today is often based on the need to make money, Indian music is for the most part based on philosophical and religious ideas. In addition, few people in India own TVs or CD players, and therefore the principal means of entertainment is through the radio, film, and live performance.

## Shimmery music

In the 1950s Ali Akbar Khan (b. 1922) and Ravi Shankar (b. 1920) brought their stringed instruments—the sarod and the sitar—to the U.S. and began to introduce the classical music of northern India. Among those first attracted to the shimmery sound, both calming and exciting, were jazz and rock musicians, including such groups as the Beatles.

But the sound already had a very long history. An Indian instrument

42

Right: Ravi Shankar has been crucial in bringing the music of the sitar to the ears of Western listeners.

modern sitar and founded Indian classical music. For many centuries afterward musical scholarship and skill were passed from father to son through family schools known as *gharanas*. The Hindus came to share with the Muslims the use of this music in their own religion, and the Indian classical music of today knows no religious differences.

## Ragas

As boys, both Ravi Shankar and Ali Akbar Khan had to learn, without the help of printed music, 72 **scales** and hundreds of compositions, called ragas (or rags), based on those scales. Unlike Western scales, which have only 12 **tones** (including **sharps** and **flats**), Indian scales have 22 microtones, which are like fractions of a sharp or flat. Since microtones can not be played on a piano, they are part of what makes Indian music sound different from Western music. Boys like Shankar and Khan also had to learn to play their instruments very well, including how to "bend" or

called the *vina*, which is the common ancestor of both the sarod and the sitar, dates back at least as far as 500 B.C. The musical forms performed on these three instruments were taken to India from Persia (present-day Iran) in the 14th century, when Muslims ruled much of both countries.

An Indo-Persian poet from that period named Amir Khusrau (1253–1325) is said to have created the

# THE SAROD AND THE SITAR

The sitar is made from teak with a gourd (an inedible fruit with a hard rind) at its base, where the sound resonates. It has a long fingerboard (the part of a stringed instrument where the fingers press down on the strings to produce different pitches), four main strings on which melodies are played, and 13 so-called sympathetic strings underneath those four, which vibrate in "sympathy" with the melody. The sarod also has four main strings but a larger number of sympathetic strings, a shorter fingerboard, and a lower, more mellow tone than the sitar. Another stringed instrument, the *tambura*, provides a drone (a single constant tone) heard behind the other Indian instruments. Some groups feature a singer. Unlike Western classical music, the Indian kind is not written down but is learned by ear and example from a master. While traditionally teacher and pupil were father and son, in modern times this is not always the case. Sometimes

the teacher is also a guru, which is a kind of religious or spiritual teacher. Both Ravi Shankar and Ali Akbar Khan, for example, studied both music and religion with Baba Allauddin Khan (1862–1972), who was also the father of both Ali Akbar Khan and Shankar's first wife.

**Below: Ali Akbar Khan—master of the sarod.**

slide into or out of tones, and how to **tune** the strings differently for each different raga. Only very recently have girls been allowed to engage in this kind of study.

At each performance the raga that is selected to be played may depend on a number of things, including mood, time of day, and the season of the year. At the start of each raga—which used to last up to an hour but may be briefer nowadays—the tones are chosen and explored by the stringed instruments. Later the raga's special **tempo** and beat (called the *tala*) are played on a pair of high-**pitched** hand drums called tabla, which accompany the melody instruments. Toward the end of the raga the pace picks up, and the music becomes very energetic. Another difference from Western classical music is that some amount of **improvisation** (free musical experimentation) is allowed, but only within the strict rules of the raga.

### Changing the rules

For centuries classical musicians played only for the nobility of India, who were rich enough to employ them and to have the time to listen to

them. But the power of the nobility declined during the 20th century, as it has in much of the world, and musicians and their audiences had to find new ways of getting together. One way became the *mahfil*, an invitation-only gathering of music lovers who pay the performers a great deal of money for the privilege of having them perform, a practice that is still an important part of the Indian music scene today. Another has been public concerts, which put the performers farther away from their

## *Public concerts have enabled more people to hear Indian music*

audience—especially in larger halls—but has the advantage of enabling more people to hear the music, including people outside India via recordings and TV. CDs have served a similar purpose and have allowed longer ragas to be recorded than was possible with the old long-playing records (LPs).

These changes have brought others. Ali Akbar Khan has set up a college in northern California for the study of north Indian classical music, and his students have included many non-Indians and players of other kinds of music. Ravi Shankar, who has a home in southern California, has taught his own students privately, including George Harrison (b. 1943) of the Beatles. One of Shankar's star sitar pupils is his own young daughter, Anoushka (b. 1981), a sign that the traditional ban on women is beginning to lift. Khan has also recorded with jazz musicians, as has tabla **virtuoso** Zakir Hussain (b. 1951), formerly the director of

**Below: Only recently have girls been allowed to engage in the study of musical instruments like the sitar and the sarod.**

**Above: Ex-Beatle George Harrison (right) at a press conference in London's Royal Festival Hall in 1970. With him are seven top Indian performers including Ravi Shankar (third from the right). They were advertising a charity concert for famine victims in Bangladesh.**

**Right: Tabla virtuoso Zakir Hussain was taught to play in the traditional way by his father Alla Rakha.**

percussion at Khan's college and the son of Alla Rakha (b. 1919), tabla player with Shankar's group. Shankar has composed for and performed with Western classical orchestras, and has also written music for the movies.

### Karnatak

The classical music of southern India, called *karnatak*, is based on similar musical principles as the north but differs in certain interesting details. Some say the differences are based on the stronger influence of Islamic culture on northern India. *Karnatak* is not as well-known in the U.S. and Europe, but some listeners from those areas like it better because it seems less strict and more exciting to them.

Some of the differences are in the instruments used in the south. They include the *vina*, which is related to

music, including bhangra from the area of Punjab, and are associated with country rituals and celebrations.

## Music from "Bollywood"

The most popular music in India, sometimes called *filmi*, has involved some of the world's most recorded singers such as Lata Mangeshkar (b. 1928), with over 30,000 songs to her name, closely followed by her younger sister Asha Bhosle (b. 1932). This music is associated with the famous film industry centered on the city of Bombay.

*Filmi* began in the 1930s when early movie stars were expected to be able to sing as well as act. However, by the 1960s the actors were merely expected to mime to the recorded voices of female singers like Bhosle and Mangeshkar, and their male counterparts such as Mohammed Rafi and Murkesh, who were called "playback singers."

Most of the movies coming out of Bombay, which became known as "Bollywood" (Bombay's answer to Hollywood) were, and still are, simple romances and adventures intended to entertain common people all over India. The songs, released as singles, often became more popular than the films and blasted from portable radios and tape players everywhere. Some songs were called film-*ghazals* because of their take-off on that ancient form of romantic musical poetry. Recent *ghazals* have dressed up tradition with **disco** beats and electric instruments.

## Music of the Sufis

Pakistan was part of northern India until it became a separate country in 1947, partly because of

the sitar but has no "sympathetic strings" (see box on page 43); the oboelike (but much longer) *nadasvaram*; and the *mridangam*, a double-headed drum. The Western violin has also been brought into play, and songs with **lyrics** are more common than in northern India.

The classical Indian musicians of today often include in their concerts a few "light classical pieces," which are shorter and not as strictly structured as ragas, and are generally felt to be relaxing and fun. *Thumri*, a light classical composition in the form of a love song, began in the 19th century, and is often played at the end of a concert. *Ghazal* songs are much older, having probably arrived in India five or six centuries earlier. Many of the earliest texts for *ghazal* are, like *thumri*, love poems. The **rhythms** of *ghazal* are now sometimes taken from Indian folk

**Above: The *vina* (or *veena*) has gourd sound boxes at each end of the fretboard and is one of the key instruments of *karnatak* music.**

**Below: The *mridangam*—a double-headed drum—is widely used in south Indian classical music.**

**Left: A Bombay street scene shows posters advertising the latest movies.**

the desire of its Muslims for a nation separate from the Hindus. *Ghazal* has some history in Pakistan, but more popular worldwide is *qawwali* (pronounced, "ka-wah-lee"). Traced back to the Persian Amir Khusrau, who was responsible for so much Indian music, *qawwali* became an expression of a special sect of Muslims called Sufis, who believe that the excitement generated by music and dance can help connect musicians and their listeners with God.

Nowadays *qawwali* is performed publicly and is not just a private religious experience. It is extremely

# THE BHANGRA BEAT

Since the early 1970s young Asians living in Britain have been more interested in a modern form of the Punjabi bhangra folk music, updated during the era of disco with synthesizers and drum machines added to the traditional instruments. Bhangra is good music to dance to, and the lyrics are often fun as well. This music has proved to be a huge success, with sales in the hundreds of thousands.

Traditionally bhangra was a music celebrating the end of the hemp (*bhang*) harvest, and it is from this word that the name bhangra derives. It was accompanied only by a *dhol*, a large barrellike drum played with a heavy stick, which gave the music its distinctive loping beat. This rhythm also characterizes today's bhangra beat, though the *dhol* has now been replaced by the *dholak*—a double-headed drum played with fingers and palms. The music was taken to Britain by South Asians who relocated there and was played at weddings and other community events. As the community began to assert itself, the music became an important symbol of its identity. Its Asian feel allowed people from different backgrounds and religions to share in a common interest.

Since bhangra is a young person's music, it is tied to fashion and trends, and so developed quickly. Bhangra bands started to add electronic instruments to the traditional ones. The new music has developed so far that many critics feel it should no longer bear the name bhangra. Recent hits by acts

**Above: Multi-instrumentalist Talvin Singh is one of a whole range of new Asian stars on Britain's music scene.**

such as Cornershop and Talvin Singh—although Asian in origin—have few of the characteristics of bhangra, but there is no doubt that its popularity will see Asian music entering the mainstream of British music in the 21st century.

Left: Nusrat Fateh Ali Khan (left) was one of the most powerful *qawwali* singers in the world. His popularity stretched farther outside his own country than that of many other Asian artists.

exciting to watch, especially since it involves the lead singer in strong vocal and physical expression. The responsibility of becoming a lead singer is often passed between male members of a family, as in classical music from north India. The singer is backed by secondary singers and musicians, who are called a "party." The party plays a miniature reed organ called the harmonium; they

---

## *Sufis believe that music can help connect musicians and listeners with God*

---

clap, drum (sometimes on tabla), and sing a repeating **chorus**. Most famous of recent *qawwali* singers was Nusrat Fateh Ali Khan (1948–1997), who toured the U.S. and elsewhere, and was featured on a couple of U.S. film soundtracks as well as recording with Michael Brook, a U.S. **avant-garde** musician, and the British band Massive Attack. Since his death his

nephew Rahat Fateh Ali Khan (b. 1973) has carried on in his place, with other family members filling out the party.

### Caste music

Nepal, a mountainous kingdom of long traditions and many religions, sits between India and Tibet, and shows influences from both places in its music. The traditions include the separation of people into castes who must obey the rules of their particular place in society and perform certain tasks. One caste travels from house to house singing for their supper and accompanying themselves on four-stringed fiddles called *sarangi*. Another caste mixes tailoring with playing for weddings and religious ceremonies on loud drums, cymbals, horns, and the shawm—an ancestor of the oboe. Blacksmiths play a piece of metal lodged between their teeth, which in its Western form is called a jew's harp. In Nepal's Kathmandu Valley both Hindu and Buddhist ceremonies involve singing and playing, with instruments assigned to

particular castes, including drums, cymbals, shawms, and flutes. The music becomes even louder at annual festivals honoring the gods of the major religions and nature.

## Nomadic music

Farther west, bordered by Iran, Pakistan, China, India, and the Central Asian republics of the former Soviet Union, Afghanistan has music that is as complex in its range of influences as that of Nepal. The Indian influence shows up in Afghans' affection for *ghazal*. Many Afghans, particularly the Pashtun ethnic group, are also nomads, meaning that they move seasonally from one part of the country to another. It is therefore no surprise that they enjoy the sort of story songs that could be sung around a campfire. These songs are accompanied by the *rebab* and *tambur*, short-necked stringed lutes; the *sarinda*, which is played with a bow; the *surnai* oboe; and the *dhol*.

Below: Over the past few years the ruling Taliban party in Afghanistan has tried to discourage people from listening to Western music by confiscating CDs and cassettes considered "unsuitable." This guardpost by the side of the road shows how serious their intentions are.

Afghans, Tadjiks, and Uzbeks have their own kinds of folk music, performed in teahouses on their own types of lute—the plucked *dambura* or the bowed *ghichak*. They also have a formal classical music heard in private homes and played on yet another kind of lute, the two-stringed, plucked *dutar*.

Before 1950 musicians, though popular, were not given much respect in Afghan society. However, the arrival of radio changed all that, and professional musicians began to flourish. Radio also meant that people from one part of the country were exposed to the music of another.

Unfortunately, conflict among the Afghans has been an excuse for ongoing fighting before and after Soviet troops invaded in 1979 and departed 10 years later. The country's Islamic rulers have discouraged the participation of women in music-making as well as making it clear that it does not approve of Western music. It seems clear that until the fighting ends, there is little hope for the prospects of music in Afghanistan.

# CHAPTER 5

# Flavors of the East

Covering countries from Indonesia to Japan, the Far East produces an enormous amount of different music, most of it far removed from Western musical tradition. However, contemporary Indonesian music is making itself heard around the world.

Many different musics are heard across the huge continent of Asia and its offshore island nations, but few of them have become very familiar in the West or had much influence on Western music. One of the most popular in recent times, however, has been created by the gamelans of Indonesia, particularly from the islands of Bali and Java.

The word "gamelan" is used to refer to a large group of instrumental players. It is also used to describe all the instruments used in gamelan

music collectively, as well as the music itself. Gamelans were used in Hindu and Buddhist ceremonies (Indonesia's main religions), and this continued even after Muslims took control of Indonesia, apart from Bali, in about 1500. There has been written music for gamelan for more than 100 years. The melodies are played on a group of metallophones—which look like xylophones but are made of metal—in **scales** of four, five, or seven **tones**.

The underlying beat, which changes dramatically from time to

**Above: A typical gamelan orchestra from the Indonesian island of Bali will include gongs, pipes, drums, and metallophones.**

time, is played on drums. Gongs are used to punctuate the melodies. The group may also include the *rebab* (a two-stringed fiddle), *suling* (a bamboo flute), and *siter* or *celempung* (types of zither).

## Gamelan performance

Gamelans are used to accompany night-time shadow-puppet plays called *wayang kulit*. The groups also perform during ceremonies and festivals, usually in connection with poetry, dance, or drama.

Many villages have their own gamelan groups, which differ from one another in both the **tuning** of their instruments and the detail of the performances. The gamelans compete in national contests, as well as for the attention of tourists. Although sultans no longer rule Indonesia, some of the best gamelans continue to perform at the royal courts in Yogyakarta and Surakarta. One of the most famous of the gamelan **choreographers** and composers is Bagong Kussudiardja (b. 1930) from Yogyakarta.

A popular and exciting ceremony that takes place on Bali is the *kecak* (pronounced "keh-chak"), known in English as the "Monkey Chant." It features dozens of men seated in circles, chattering away to represent the monkey army that helped King Rama, a Hindu god, rescue his queen from an evil ogre. The **interludes** are played by a gamelan.

## Traditional Chinese music

Unlike Indonesia, where music has been allowed to flourish, Chinese music has been restrained by its communist government, particularly during the so-called Cultural Revolution (1966–1976), when Western influences were forbidden and traditional forms of music were discouraged. Yet many of the

# CHINESE OPERA

**Left: Though its popularity has not traveled, opera remains hugely popular in China.**

Unlike Western operas, which are generally known by their composers, Chinese operas are usually known by the region from which they come. There are operas being performed just about everywhere in China throughout the year, but among the many different regional forms Peking opera is by far the most popular.

Peking opera is made up of singing accompanied by an orchestra, broken up by spoken sections. The main instruments in the orchestra are *hu-ch'in* (bowed two-stringed instruments) and a number of plucked stringed instruments, such as the *pipa* and the three-stringed, long-necked *san-hsien*. Percussion is provided by drums, gongs, clappers, and cymbals. The music uses two main musical styles—*erh-huang*, for the serious sections of the drama, and *hsi-p'i*, for lively and happy sections.

The actors use many complex gestures, each of which has a specific meaning. For example, to express anger, the actor will move backward and throw his sleeves out below his waist, and to portray a flirtatious girl, the actor will adopt a wavering walk. Until the 20th century all of the women in Peking opera were played by men or boys, called *tans*. Boys from the age of seven were recruited from Peking and received strict training for these roles. The stories used in Peking opera are either about love and social matters, called *wen* operas, or military and heroic adventures, which are called *wu* operas. Since the communist government took power in 1949, it has encouraged composers to write operas about the everyday lives of people living under communism, and it is these types of operas that are performed most often today.

precommunist traditional music forms survived, especially in remote villages.

China has its own classical music and opera, both of which have little or nothing to do with Western **harmony** and **orchestration**. They make use of a pear-shaped lute called the *pipa* (see Volume 1, page 8) and zithers called the *zheng* and *qin*. However, Chinese composers have often used the violin and cello in their pieces. Since the late

18th and 19th centuries Western music has had a significant presence in China, influencing the development of indigenous forms of music in dramatic ways. Since the Cultural Revolution all institutions, traditions, and practices of Western classical music have been nurtured in China, to the point where China is producing some of the most promising **virtuoso** Western classical instrumentalists in the world.

Some of China's folk music is kept alive around the country by groups called "silk-and-bamboo" ensembles. They sometimes gather in teahouses to play a variety of Chinese versions of the fiddle, flute, and banjo. Ritual music performed by priests of the Taoist religion takes place in religious temples and at weddings and funeral ceremonies in some areas of the countryside. One of the traditional instruments used in ritual music is the *sheng*—a large "mouth organ" with

**Above: The powerful Kodo drummers are one of the most successful musical exports from Japan.**

**Below: The *pipa*— a pear-shaped lute —is often used to perform traditional Chinese music.**

many tall reeds that are arranged in a circle. It sounds like a harmonica (see Volume 1, pages 6 and 8).

## Musics of Japan

The classical Japanese music most famous in the West is performed on the *shakuhachi* (a breathy-sounding bamboo flute) and the *koto* (a large 13-stringed zither that is played horizontally). One form of Japanese classical music, *gagaku*, is more than 1,200 years old. It uses a range of 20 instruments, including the *shô* (a reed-pipe mouth organ similar to the Chinese *sheng*), flutes, chimes, drums, and gongs. *Gagaku* is now performed mainly at the Imperial Court in Kyoto. Music also accompanies the *noh* and *kabuki* styles of traditional theater.

The most important Japanese folk music events are the *bon odori* festivals, held during the summer throughout Japan. Contrasting sounds come from the gentle *shakuhachi* and from groups of huge, loud, barrel-shaped *taiko* drums, with the drummers dancing and shouting while they play.

Another ancient Japanese form of music is *min'yo*—a folk music first sung by *geishas* (female hostesses) but now performed by village people at an upbeat **tempo**. They play the music on the *shamisen*, which resembles a banjo and produces a sharp, clapping sound. One of the greatest stars of modern *min'yo* is the singer Takio Ito

# ASIAN THROAT SINGING

So-called "throat-singing," found in the steppes of Central Asia west of China, has been one of the biggest Asian hits in the West. Called *xoomei* (pronounced "who-may") in the language of Tuva, its most famous location, throat-singing allows one singer to produce two or even three notes at the same time, above or below the main melody note. This is done by vibrating more than just the vocal cords used in ordinary singing, applying special tension, and causing the sound to echo using the mouth as a sound box—a hollow space in which sound reverberates. Performers from the Republic of Tuva, of whom the most famous is the group Huun-Huur-Tu, accompany themselves by strumming on long-necked *doshpuluurs* and plucking the *xomuz*—a form of jew's harp—while they sing about horses (which have great importance in the lives of the people) or about the people and places they love. Throat-singing is also found in Mongolia, east of Tuva.

**Left: A member of the group Huun-Huur-Tu with a *doshpuluur*.**

from Hokkaido island, north of the Japanese mainland. He and his band Tryin' Times helped revolutionize *min'yo* by adding Western electric instruments to the traditional *shamisen*, *taiko*, and *shakuhachi*.

One of the oldest Japanese pop forms is *enka*, which by the 1920s had begun to use the sounds of Western scales as well as traditional Japanese **minor modes**. One of the main *enka* modes, called *Yo*, is made up of the notes A, C, D, E, G, A.

A dramatic singing style and the ability to create a strong emotional atmosphere are the most important elements in *enka*. Singers of *enka* developed a tearful crying sound in their voices by using **vibrato**—a fluttering of the voice higher or lower in **pitch** than the main note—as they sang about life's sadness. The singer Misora Hibari (1937–1989) is Japan's most well-known *enka* star, recording 500 records in her lifetime. She was

**Yo Mode**

**Below left: The *Yo* mode—used in *enka* music—is made up of the notes A, C, D, E, G, and octave A. Below: Takio Ito (left) and his band Tryin' Times playing live in Japan in 1999. Their use of both old and modern instruments results in traditional music with a fresh new sound.**

followed by the current star Miyako Harumi, who has also used her virtuoso voice as an unusual addition to modern rock groups.

Modern bands that blend *min'yo*, festival music, salsa, **reggae**, and pop from elsewhere in Asia are called *kayokyoku*, meaning "fusion." The Japanese island of Okinawa, more than 300 miles south of the mainland, has been particularly successful at creating great dancehall **rhythms** while keeping the sound of *min'yo* and other Japanese traditions alive.

# CHAPTER 6

# The Islamic World

The Arabs had a long history of music before the Islamic religion took root in the area now known as the Middle East in the seventh century. Although Islam preaches that music is a sin, music has continued to thrive in the Islamic world.

The Arabs, who were mostly nomads (meaning they had no permanent homes), have a long history of music. In ancient times female slaves accompanied Arab warriors, singing and dancing while playing the tabla (the ancestor of the Indian drum) or the *duff* (an early tambourine). Then Islam, one of the world's main religions, began among the Arabic people living in the area now known as the Middle East— between Europe, Africa, and Asia—in the seventh century. Islam preaches

**Above: A muezzin calls the people to prayer at the mosque. Although Islam does not officially recognize the role of music in its religious rituals, it could be said that the muezzin is making ancient Arabic music, even though Muslims would not call it that.**

that music is a sin, and both singing and playing instruments were banned. Yet away from the mosques, in the Arab courts, music was allowed to thrive, since those in power found it to be a great source of pleasure. Despite the strict attitude of Muslims (followers of Islam) who condemn it, music has continued to develop through the centuries, sometimes as a protest against Islamic doctrine.

## Arab music moves west

Soon after adopting Islam, the Arabs went westward out of the Middle East through northern Africa, and then across to Spain and Portugal to spread their new religion. Although music was frowned on, the Arab invaders, far from the disapproving ears of their Islamic preachers, created songs about their faith. This music took hold in northern Africa and Spain, where it came to sound different from other music that would develop in Europe and in the rest of Africa.

The differences have partly to do with the **modes** used in Arab music, which seem to slide from **minor** to **major** and back, and depend on fractions of **intervals** smaller than the half-steps, or **semitones**, in which European instruments are **tuned**. For example, a **tone** in Arabic music may be halfway between an F and an F-sharp. It can be sung or played on an Arabic string instrument, but not on a Western piano, since it would be somewhere between a white and a black note on the keyboard.

The Arab invaders brought along their own instruments to accompany the singers or to play solo or in groups. They plucked and bowed strings, blew into reeds and flutes, and shook and pounded **rhythms** on drums, tambourines, and cymbals. These instruments were the ancestors of many Western instruments.

## The beat of the Berbers

Before the arrival of the Arabs, the Berbers lived in North Africa. They managed to keep their own religion and their own flutes and drums when they retreated from the Arabs into the mountains of what is now Morocco.

Many Moors, of mixed Arab and Berber blood, crossed the Strait of Gibraltar and settled in the region of Andalusia in southern Spain. Using certain rules of composition and rhythm, they developed their own music. It influenced the dancing gypsies of Spain and became what is today known as flamenco. Flamenco

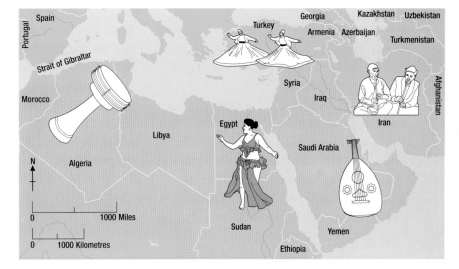

**Above: The Islamic world—located in an area containing parts of Europe, North Africa, and Asia— reaches west to Morocco and east to Iran (ancient Persia) and the southern republics of the former Soviet Union.**

**Below: An *andaluz* orchestra in Morocco features such Arabic instruments as the oud (right).**

music, based on vocals and guitars, is accompanied by a spirited dance in which the dancers add to the rhythm by stamping their feet and playing castanets (two small, spoon-shaped pieces of wood held in the palm of the hand and between the fingers that make a clicking sound when struck together). When the Moors were forced out of Spain by the Christians in the 14th century, they took their music—called *andaluz*—back to northern Africa, where it developed into a variety of new musics.

Today Morocco is largely Muslim, but Berber drumming groups still exist. In neighboring Algeria *andaluz* has been adopted into *rai*, which is popular with young North Africans in clubs and dancehalls. Its youth appeal is partly because of the rebellion of its music and **lyrics** against strict aspects of Islam, including discrimination against women. *Rai* music uses the electronic instruments, synthesizers, and percussion of rock music, while holding onto Arabic rhythms and modes. Cheb Khaled (b. 1960) and Chaba Fadela (b. 1962) are among the most well-known singers of *rai*.

## Egyptian music

Music is an essential part of everyday life in Egypt, accompanying weddings and café life with the sounds of the

*nay* (a breathy-sounding flute), *rebab* (a bowed, two-stringed instrument) and *mazhar* (a type of clarinet), and the violin and brass instruments introduced by the European colonials. The percussion instruments used are the tabla or *darabuka* (a single-skin drum beaten with both hands), *reque* (a wooden tambourine with five to eight cymbals), and *sagat* (cymbals).

Belly-dancing, or *raks sharki*, began as an exercise to strengthen women before childbirth. The dance depends on a complex, formal style of music, performed by Egyptian **virtuosos** on some of the above-mentioned melody and percussion instruments.

As elsewhere in northern Africa, modern Egyptian youths have sought a musical means of expressing their passions and criticisms. It is called *shaabi* ("of the people") because of its roots among working people. Ahmed Adaweyah, a sort of Egyptian soul

**Right: Cheb Khaled was the first *rai* star to have his music released in Europe, when a British label decided to put out one of his albums in the mid-1980s.**

**Below: A man sells *rebabs* (Arabic two-stringed instruments played with a bow) in Philae, Egypt.**

singer, is one of the top *shaabi* stars. There is also *al-jil* ("generation") music, which is danceable and hyped up electronically, with Arabic vocal **arrangements** and rhythms. One of those who helped develop *al-jil* music is a Libyan named Hamid el-Shaeri, who went to Egypt in 1974. He worked with Egyptian musicians to create this new sound and had a huge hit with his song "Lolaiki" in 1988.

### Sounds of Sudan and Ethiopia

Sudan, located along the White Nile River south of Egypt, is musically Arabic in the north, but echoes the rhythms and percussion of nearby Kenya and Uganda in the south. Some Sudanese wedding dances have a unique form of vocal and drum accompaniment: lyrics praising the bride and groom are **improvised** to the sound of women drumming.

Hamza el-Din (b. 1929), born in the northern Nubian region of Sudan that is shared with Egypt, brought world attention to his adaptations of Sudanese folk music. Dividing his home between Japan and California, he plays the oud (a plucked Arabic lute) and the *tar* (large tambourine). Many Sudanese performers, such as singer and oud-player Mohamed al-Amin and singer Mohamed Wardi, have had to leave Sudan to get their music heard and recorded. Since the National Islamic Front military regime took power in 1989, it has persecuted Sudanese musicians.

Ethiopia, east of Sudan, shares the basic pentatonic **scale** (see page 24) with its neighbor. The Ethiopian soul music known as Amharic has a beautiful sound, with widely spaced intervals, slithering rhythms, and twists of language. This mix of elements led to the singer-and-band groups of the 1970s and, after a 1980s dictatorship, a generation of young Ethiopian singer-songwriters at home and in exile abroad who stirred global interest in their music. The most successful is singer Aster Aweke (b. 1961), who fled to the U.S. in 1979, where she still performs.

---

## *Ethiopia shares the basic pentatonic scale with its neighbor Sudan*

---

Meanwhile, the folk sounds of the *kebero* (drums), *washint* (flute), and *krar* (a harp that resembles an ancient Greek instrument) and the wiggles of the *tchik-tchik-ka* dance and its rhythmic horn and synthesizer music continue to be heard and seen in the clubs of the capital city, Addis Ababa.

### The power of Persia and Turkey

The instruments and musical forms of North Africa reappear, with variations, in the rest of the Islamic world, which extends north and east through Saudi Arabia, Yemen, Iran, Iraq, Turkey, and the southern republics of the former Soviet Union. Many of these instruments, such as the *kamancheh*—a spiked fiddle that is bowed while the spike rests on the ground—probably

originated among Persians in the area of present-day Iran and Turkey before the arrival of the Arabs or the Islamic religion. They later formed the basis for many European instruments.

Persian classical music, based on *dastgahs*—collections of melodic modes similar to ragas (see pages 43–44), which *dastgahs* influenced—is still performed in Iran. *Dastgahs* are specially chosen to match the season and time of day of a performance.

Turkey has many regional folk styles, as well as *fasil*—a light vocal music usually accompanied by the *klarnet* (a type of clarinet) that is played by gypsies in city restaurants.

## WHIRLING DERVISHES

One Islamic sect, the Sufis, holds a different view about music from most Muslims. The Sufis believe that through music and dance a believer reaches the divine. Sufis march and play to celebrate saints' days in Egypt, bringing some of their listeners to a state of ecstasy. In Turkey Sufi dervishes whirl in circles to put themselves into a divine trance accompanied by the energetic and spiritual sounds of *neys* (the Turkish version of Egyptian *nays*), *kanuns* (zithers), *rebabs*, violins, and singers. The main performances of this music take place from December 3 to 17 every year at the Mevlana festival in Konya, Turkey. The whirling dervishes went from Turkey to Sudan a few centuries ago, where their dance and music have also taken root. The most wild dervish music, driven by exciting drum rhythms, has been taken up by the Sudanese *zar* cult—a female religious group that dances from dawn to dusk to release pent-up frustrations in sessions lasting up to seven days.

**Right: The dervishes dance with one hand pointed up and the other down to maintain a balance between heaven and the earth.**

## CHAPTER 7

# Africa

With its infectious traditional melodies and complex drum rhythms, backed by modern electric instruments, African music has become popular all over the world. To understand this music, it is essential to examine its native African roots.

**Below: A young drummer in Burundi —drums are the instruments most closely associated with African music.**

Africa has a rich and ancient musical history. Its soulful and inspired vocals, motivating **rhythms**, and imaginative instruments have deeply influenced the music of many different countries. This musical impact has its origins in the late 15th and 16th centuries, when Columbus discovered the "New World," and the English, French Spanish, and Portuguese began

to transport Africans from the western and central regions of the continent to work as slaves in the Caribbean and Americas. Those enslaved Africans took their music with them, and played a vital part in the development of many musical styles in the New World—from salsa and **samba** to blues and jazz. To understand many of these musics, it is important to go back to their African roots.

Since the 16th century African music has obviously developed in many different directions. However, many of the older traditional forms have survived in one form or another. A number of West Africa's best-known musicians are related to noble families of precolonial African kingdoms and to the griots, who were the court musicians and historians in those kingdoms. The descendants of griots (sometimes called *jalis*) are spread throughout the present-day countries of Senegal, Guinea, Guinea-Bissau, and Gambia on the Atlantic coast and the larger land-locked nation of Mali.

**West Africa**
West African musicians, such as Mory Kante (b. 1956) from Guinea, and Baaba Maal (b. 1952) and Youssou N'Dour (b. 1959) from Senegal, play

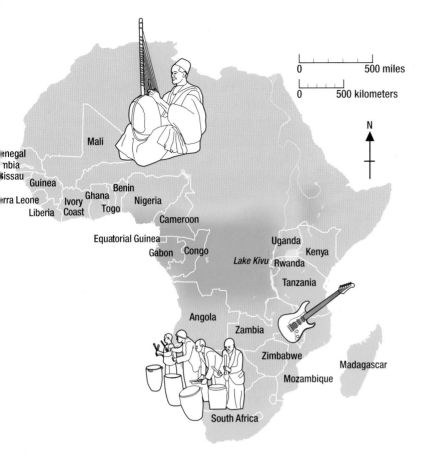

drums, highlife is great music to dance to. Indeed, that is how the music got its name. In Ghana performers of highlife added guitars to the traditional instruments of the *kora* and the West African talking drum. After World War II they added Euro-American dance-band instruments. The later influence of rock 'n' roll brought electrified instruments and electronic keyboards into the mix. Nigeria contributed other dance rhythms and some of highlife's most popular performers of the 1950s and 1960s.

The music of the Yoruba tribe from southwestern Nigeria has been affected by Arabic influences from the north and Brazilian and European influences from across the seas. Men gathering in seacoast cafés after work to drink, sing, and play developed "palm-wine" music—gentle music accompanied by acoustic guitars and generally sung in English. Brazil contributed a tambourine, which led to a form of palm-wine music called *juju*, with stringed instruments backed by gentle, breezy percussion.

modern **arrangements** of ancient melodies. They use electric instruments with rhythmic influences from the Caribbean and the Americas. Such artists have toured the world with this exciting and danceable mix, and are popular worldwide.

Ali Farka Touré (b. 1939) is a native of northern Mali. His technical mastery of the guitar and the sad melodies he writes have attracted American blues musicians—such as guitarists Taj Mahal and Ry Cooder— to record with him.

**Above: The continent of Africa. This map shows the countries where indigenous (local) music remains strong. The countries to the north and east produce music influenced by the Islamic world (see Chapter 6).**

## The high life
The most popular musical style in many parts of Africa is "highlife." It originated in West Africa and is now centered in the former British colonies of Ghana and Nigeria. Yet its roots lie in Sierra Leone, Guinea's neighbor to the south, where former slaves who escaped from Jamaica took their guitars and songs early in the 19th century.

With its light guitar melodies over a strong rhythm played by bass and

**Right: Senegal's Youssou N'Dour was the most successful African artist in Europe during the 1990s. His song "7 Seconds" reached No. 3 on the U.K. charts in 1994.**

Above: The master *kora* player Tourmani Diabate has often toured in Europe and America.

## THE *KORA*

Many griots accompany their singing with a large decorated instrument called the *kora*. It resembles a lute or a guitar, with 21 strings along a neck without **frets**. The strings, which stretch over a gourd **resonator** or sound box covered with animal skin, are plucked by the thumb and forefinger of each hand. The clear sound resembles a harp. The remaining fingers grip two vertical hand posts. The strings are made of fishing line, which provides a brilliant **tone**, and players use a variety of different **tunings**. Griots also play the *ngoni*, similar to a lute, and the *balafon*—a form of xylophone—which is made of tuned bars of wood and struck with mallets.

many traditional musics in West Africa. For example, Ghana has encouraged the booming drum ensembles of the coastal Ga tribe and the xylophones of the northern Lobi. Nigeria's tribes—at times at war with each other—have their own individual musical forms, often influenced by one another.

The Mandinka empire, centered in Mali, once extended to the land of the Hausa in present-day northern Nigeria. Songs of praise sung to noblemen and ensembles of xylophone, percussion, and *goje* (a one-stringed fiddle) are still heard in this area, sounding a bit like the music of the griots further north in Senegal. The Hausa's trumpet, the *kakalai*, also dates back to the empire. Similar instruments are found among the Igbo tribesmen of the southeast, where music accompanies rituals and ceremonies of the traditional chiefs, and a zither called the *obo* is strummed during more informal occasions.

The music of Wassoulou, south of the Malian capital of Bamako, lies outside the griot tradition. It has its own unique pentatonic (five-note) **modes** and instruments, including the *donsongoni* (a 5-stringed oblong

King Sunny Adé (b. 1946) has electrified his large *juju* group, which often tours around the world.

The studios of the Ivory Coast have served as a recording site for much of West Africa, and the country is also the home of international dancehall dynamo Alpha Blondy (b. 1953). Benin, wedged with Togo between Ghana and Nigeria, has produced another global favorite, singer Angélique Kidjo (b. 1960). While making use of modern electronics and special effects, she also uses touches of traditional tribal drum rhythms and melodies in her songs.

### Traditional music

Despite the influence of Western music in former British colonies such as Ghana and Nigeria, there are still

Below: King Sunny Adé and his *juju* band in concert in Paris, France, in 1996.

lute) and *kamalengoni* (a harplike instrument much smaller than the *kora*), and the *fle*, a gourd strung with shells. Women performers are featured much more in this region than in the rest of West Africa.

Even more distinct from the rest of West Africa is the tiny nation of Cape Verde—a collection of islands 400 miles off the coast of Senegal. Since Cape Verde was a colony of Portugal until 1975, it is no surprise to hear the sad Portuguese **ballad** form called *fado* echoed in the songs and dance forms of the islands, although there is more sway and **syncopation** in Cape Verde's music. This magical music has

Above: Les Têtes Brulées from Cameroon have blended rock and traditional music to form their own brand of *bikutsi*.

---

## It is no surprise to hear the Portuguese-style ballad form called fado in Cape Verde

---

been made familiar through the clear and beautiful voice of a cigar-smoking, whiskey-drinking Cape Verdean grandmother named Cesaria Evora (b. 1941), who plays to packed concert halls around the world.

### Les Têtes Brulées
Located where the African continent makes a turn to the south and next to Nigeria, the country of Cameroon uses the talking drum and *balafon* found among its northern neighbors, as well as the thumb piano or *mbira* (an instrument made up of tuned metal strips with a gourd resonator) found further south in Zimbabwe. There are also instruments brought by Europeans during the time when it was a colony of Germany, Britain, and France. Cameroonians dance to the moderate **tempo** of *makossa*, as well as to the speedier sound of *bikutsi*, the tribal source of which lies with

the *balafons* of the Beti deep in the interior rainforest. Both these dance forms have been updated in recent years, most notably by Les Têtes Brulées (which means "The Burning Heads" in French). Formed from musicians and writers living in the capital city of Yaounde, Les Têtes were as attracted to the primal energy of the Beti as they were to the power of U.S. pop. The group has stunned audiences around the world with its bizarre hairdos, painted faces and bodies, scraps of clothing, and wild soccer-ball-kicking dance steps, performed to their brand of *bikutsi*.

### Bringing it all back home
The small former Spanish colony of Equatorial Guinea, south of Cameroon, and the even smaller, formerly Portuguese island republics of São Tomé and Príncipe have produced almost nothing in the way of recordings or touring bands. But Equatorial Guinea boasts thrilling

**choral** groups and its own variety of the palm-wine music found in Nigeria. São Tomé and Príncipe celebrate Christian and folk legends with eye-catching festivities similar to the Rio carnival in Brazil, and the inhabitants dance to electric bands like those in the Democratic Republic of Congo.

Formerly known as Zaire (and in colonial days as the Belgian Congo), the Democratic Republic of Congo, in the heart of Central Africa, has served as a source for much of the continent's and the world's musics.

## "AFRO-BEAT"

**Above: Fela Kuti, one of the greatest African music stars. He took his music and its message around the world.**

A Nigerian Yoruban, Fela Kuti (1938–1997) came up with the term "Afro-Beat" for his particular kind of West African soul music. His **lyrics**, many of which criticized his country's military dictatorships, led to him being persecuted and imprisoned in his own country for many years.

In the 1930s the favor was returned: the rhythms taken by Congolese and West African slaves to the Caribbean and America returned to the motherland in the form of Cuban **rumba**, which was adopted and reworked to form another popular musical style in Central Africa.

### Re-creating the past

Many 20th-century Congolese musicians have re-created the sounds and techniques of bow, zither, and folk violin or thumb piano on acoustic or electric guitars. Using these instruments and the traditional rhythms, they have recast the rumba as a happy dance style called *soukous*.

> *Guitar music has become incredibly popular in the Congo, Kenya, and Uganda*

Visits from rock 'n' roll and soul legend James Brown (b. 1933) in the late 1960s and early 1970s inspired the Congolese to include horns on their recordings of *soukous*, which were beginning to become hot sellers across the continent.

During the political troubles of this time some Congolese artists began to leave the country. Two of their destinations were the former British colonies of Kenya and Uganda, to the east. As a result guitar-playing became tremendously popular there, and a variety of new instrumental and singing styles developed in these countries.

As in West Africa and the Congo, some of these styles have the guitar imitating native instruments such as the *nyatiti*, a lyre from western Kenya. The Kikuyu tribe, also from Kenya, prefers guitar slides (slipping

Left: American soul
singer James Brown
spars with boxer
Muhammad Ali
during one of
Brown's many visits
to Africa during the
1960s and 1970s.
Brown's influence
on the music of the
Congo is undeniable.

are also fond of Congolese *soukous*, but the bands and audiences in Tanzania have their own way of playing it and dancing to it, which they call *mtindo*.

## Malagasy music

The large island republic of Madagascar is separated from the east coast of Africa not only by 300 miles of Indian Ocean but also by the look and sound of its people. They speak a unique language related to their backgrounds in Malaysia, in Southeast Asia, and in Polynesia in the middle of the Pacific Ocean.

Malagasy (the adjective used for things from Madagascar) music is equally unique, though it is becoming more familiar to Westerners through recordings on the U.S.-based Shanachie label and through touring pop bands such as Tarika. The islanders' fondness for jaunty accordion music is probably left over from its many years as a French colony, but what they play sounds more like Tex-Mex music from Texas. Their flute-playing sounds like Irish

the finger along a string to produce a quick, smooth change of **pitch**), which are familiar in U.S. country music, and a fast beat suggesting **rhythm and blues** or soul music.

The position of Tanzania and its tiny offshore neighbor of Zanzibar on the east coast of Africa has opened those countries to many centuries of Arab influence, shared also by the coastal parts of Kenya. Arabic roots (see Chapter 6) are heard in the **scales** and **quarter-tone intervals** of this region's music, as well as in instruments, such as the oud, the *dumbak*, and tabla, all of which are also played in northern Africa. But the 20th-century East African style called *taarab* puts a special, exciting twist on those influences. It is a form of musical poetry, sung (often by women) to rhythms suited to dance, that adds electric bass guitars and electronic keyboards to more traditional instruments. Tanzanians

Below: A *taarab* band
from Zanzibar plays
a mixture of African,
Arabic, and Western
instruments.

# MUSICAL PEOPLES

Pygmy tribes, isolated in their rainforest villages, have only recently had their amazing music exposed to the rest of the world. The pygmies are exceptionally musical people, singing at every occasion, often accompanied by rhythms played on a unique kind of water-filled drum.

The Bantu, a Congolese tribe, contributed the world-famous conga drum to **world music**. The Bashi, living in the eastern part of the region near Lake Kivu, use the *kasayi* (thumb piano), the *nzenze* (with two strings and three frets), the *lulanga* (a long, flat zither), and the *mulizi* (a flute into which the player hums while blowing).

The Bahema of Rwanda have the *ndongo* (a seven-stringed harp), while the nearby Bakoga have a single-stringed violin called the *ndingiti*, possibly related to the Arabic *rebec*. It is still heard in parts of northern Africa. Rwanda's Tutsi and Hutu tribes have both developed drumming groups, and the Hutu's *umunahi*—a hunting bow with a gourd resonator—bears a resemblance to Brazil's *berimbau*. Most tribes also have their own solo and choral vocal styles in which the roots of the blues can be heard.

**Right: A Baaka pygmy from the Central African Republic, north of the Congo, plays an instrument made from a branch and vines.**

music, while the thrilling vocals sound like they come from Hawaii or from Bulgaria. The music of Madagascar is essentially a multicultural melting pot.

Madagascar's guitarists, unlike many of those in mainland Africa, often play native instruments. One is the *valiha* (pronounced "vah-lee"), which is still played and sounds like a heavenly harp. The *valiha* is made in several different shapes, one of which looks like an old-fashioned U.S. mailbox covered with many strings. Other Malagasy instruments include the *sodina* (an end-blown flute) and long bundles of grass that are shaken as percussion. The large island's variety of music includes *salegy*—a galloping rhythm originating on the west coast—and *famadihana*, which is played at a special yearly celebration during which the Malagasy dig up their dead ancestors, dress them in fresh cloth, and dance with them.

Another unique feature of Madagascan music is that many of the instruments are made from applewood. As they are played, they warm up and produce a sweet smell, so introducing another sense into the exotic musical experience.

## Moving south

Further south, Zambia, like much of Central and East Africa, has learned to dance to *soukous*—the pop music of the Democratic Republic of Congo, its big neighbor to the north. Zambians are also fond of *kwela*—a form of jive music played on a pennywhistle—and other popular forms of music from the Republic of South Africa. Despite the Zambians love of music from other countries, Zambia's President Kaunda, who played guitar as a hobby, encouraged the development of a new national dance form in the 1970s. The result was *kalindula*, a sort of **funky** cousin of *soukous*, which was named after the country's own one-stringed bass.

Zimbabwe, one step further south, has preserved a couple of traditional instruments, the *mbira* (thumb piano) and marimba (a type of xylophone). They appear both in dancehalls and in special ceremonies, such as the *bira*, in which Zimbabweans stay up all night in an effort to reach the spirits of their ancestors through singing, chanting, and dancing.

*Soukous* reappears in Zimbabwe in a version called *rumbira*, in reference to the rumba (from Cuba) and the *mbira*. The world-famous singer and guitarist Thomas Mapfumo (b. 1949) has made use of electrified *mbiras* and has built his band's modern electric guitar style around them. This combination of sounds supports his lyrics, which contain social and political messages in a form called *chimurenga* (liberation war).

## The Portuguese effect
On either side of Zimbabwe and Zambia lie a pair of former Portuguese colonies—Angola on

**Above: Musicians playing *mbiras*. The instrument is played by plucking the tuned metal strips with the thumbs. The gourd acts as a sound resonator.**

the Atlantic Ocean to the west, and Mozambique on the Indian Ocean to the east. Angola's *kizomba* style—heavy on percussion and guitars with highlights from horns and marimba—is a little like the samba of Brazil, the former Portuguese colony on the other side of the Atlantic. The music of Mozambique is similar in its use of xylophones (which they call *timbilas*) and in its tradition-based but updated and modernized dance music called *marrabenta*.

## Black and white unite
The powerful and highly populated Republic of South Africa at the continent's southern tip has begun to share music between its black and white citizens since the removal of its apartheid policies (the separating of people from different backgrounds and races) in 1989. But black South African music had been gaining recognition outside the country for some time before that.

**Left: Thomas Mapfumo, or TM as he is known, is the most famous singer-guitarist to have emerged from Zimbabwe.**

It had its roots in the Sotho, Xhosa, and Zulu people who settled in the area between the third and 17th centuries. Their beautiful traditional choral techniques were easily adapted to the Christian gospel music that came with European colonization. During the growth of the nation's biggest cities in the 20th century black South Africans were exposed to other European and U.S. music, including jazz.

Apartheid (meaning "apartness" in Dutch) was a set of policies established by the white minority government in the late 1940s to secure power over the black majority. It separated the races and confined many blacks to township areas, so limiting their access to outside music. Blacks continued, however, to use instruments from foreign bands in simple three-**chord** music that came to be called township jive. This and other more traditional musical forms were recorded and broadcast over radio stations aimed at black neighborhoods.

The black forms of music included pennywhistle jive or *kwela*, based on the traditional reed flute-playing of cattle herders. Still more popular was and is *mbaqanga*—pronounced "im-ba-kan-ga"—which means "stew" in the Bantu language. *Mbaqanga* is a rhythmic, soulful jive with roots in 16th-century tribal wedding songs; in more recent versions it is performed with a rhythm section of bass, drums, and guitar, as well as a horn section.

The best-known and one of the longest-lived *mbaqanga* acts was Mahlathini and the Mahotella Queens, from Soweto Township. Mahlathini (1937–1999)—whose name means "Forest" in the Zulu language—sang in a groaning bass voice. He was backed by a trio of female dancer-singers whose name, Mahotella, referred to the many motels they had to stay at while touring between Pietersburg and Johannesburg.

MAHLATHINI
and the MAHOTELLA QUEENS

EARTHWORKS

THOKOZILE

Above: This CD features Mahlathini's versions of the best *mbaqanga* songs of the 1960s, 1970s, and 1980s—its success pushed the band to international stardom.

Left: Schoolboys dancing in a township near Johannesburg, South Africa. The townships were where black music flourished during the years of apartheid, when black communities had limited access to other influences.

# TOWNSHIP JAZZ

Jazz became popular in South Africa in the 1950s, particularly among blacks in the seacoast regions. This was partly due to their mixing with foreign sailors, and partly because the traditional music of the Xhosa people living there was already full of complex **harmonies** and arrangements like those found in jazz. In the townships bands favored a type of jazz called *marabi*—heavy on brass instruments, with repeated melodic phrases used over simple chords. Although *marabi* was hugely popular, some musicians, like pianist Dollar Brand (b. 1934) and trumpeter Hugh Masakela (b. 1939), became more interested in the U.S. approach to jazz. Those players and others, including vocalist Miriam Makeba (b. 1932), decided that they had to leave their country—with its apartheid restrictions—in order to develop their music. Many found fame and fortune in the U.S. and Europe. Following the lifting of apartheid, several of them have now been able to return to their homeland, so further increasing South African's musical mix.

## Outside influences

Two influences from outside South Africa helped form the music of what may be the country's most famous act, Ladysmith Black Mambazo, from Ladysmith Township. One influence was Christian gospel music, practiced by groups of Zulu men separated from their families and living in labor camps. Their singing style evolved into *iscathamiya*, which means "to step softly" and is pronounced "is-ka-ta-me-ya." This quietly uplifting and often sensuous song form is performed a capella (meaning without instruments). Joseph Shabalala (b. *c.*1940), Ladysmith's **tenor**-voice leader, claimed that the sound came to him in a dream.

The other outside influence came from U.S. singer-songwriter Paul Simon, who asked Ladysmith to perform on his best-selling 1986 album *Graceland* and on videos to promote the album. Following this, Ladysmith became well known in the West not only as a touring band and on record but also for the soundtrack of the movie *The Lion King* (1995).

**Below: Johnny Clegg and his band Savuka—one of the few South African bands to include both black and white musicians during the apartheid regime.**

## Against apartheid

While apartheid was still in force, Johnny Clegg (b. 1953) was one of the few white South African musicians to embrace black tribal styles. He helped make them popular with his band Savuka, which consists of both black and white musicians. The son of a Lithuanian Jewish mother and a Scottish father, Clegg learned Zulu music, the Zulu language, and stick fighting from street musicians in Johannesburg and their friends in the townships. He was arrested several times for disobeying apartheid laws, and his songs, often mixing Zulu and English lyrics, were a way for him to protest against apartheid.

Most white South African music written and played before apartheid catered to the Dutch and English backgrounds of the Afrikaans, the country's ruling minority, who enjoyed accordion music, European dances, and ballads. Some interest in this "safe" music continues among young Afrikaans, although increasingly many prefer to listen to the latest imported U.S. and British hits.

# TIMELINE

**c.41,000 B.C.** Musical instruments like flutes are made out of bones, shells, and sticks.

**c.10,000 B.C.** Andean peoples in South America begin playing wind and percussion instruments.

**c.3000 B.C.** Egyptians write songs and play flutes, harps, trumpets, tambourines, and drums.

**c.2000 B.C.** Pentatonic (five-note) scale is developed.

**c.1400 B.C.** The Chinese play drums, bells, flutes, and chimes.

**c.1100 B.C.** The Chinese are using the zither and a mouth organ called the *sheng*.

**c.550 B.C.** Greek philosopher Pythagoras originates the idea of notes, octaves, pitches, and scales.

**c.380 B.C.** Greek philosophers encourage music education. Instruments include the *kithara* (a lyre) and *aulos* (like an oboe).

**c.350 B.C.** Greek theorist Aristoxenus identifies rhythm, semitones, and explains scales.

**c.300 B.C.** Greek engineer Ktesibios invents the organ, using water to control the air pressure.

**c.100 A.D.** Christians sing hymns and psalms, using a solo-and-response method.

**late 500s A.D.** Pope Gregory I standardizes church music, known as Gregorian chant, or plainsong.

**700s A.D.** Moors invade Spain and southern Europe, bringing their instruments, sliding modes, and the origins of flamenco.

**c.800 A.D.** The Japanese classical music known as *gagaku* begins.

**800s A.D.** Air pumped through bellows replaces water as the means for working an organ.

**900s A.D.** Bowed instruments are brought to Europe from Asia.

**c.1025** Guido d'Arezzo invents musical notation, including staves.

**1000s–1100s** Minstrels roam Europe performing secular music.

**1100s** Organum music leads to the more complex, multiple-part music known as polyphony.

**late 1100s** Drums become a common rhythm-keeping instrument in Europe.

**1200s** In France composers adapt plainsong to invent the motet—a form of vocal polyphonic music.

**1300s** A system of harmony develops out of plainsong in France and Italy.

**early 1300s** Persian Amir Khusrau creates Indian classical music, Sufi *qawwali* music, and the sitar.

**1400s** The slide trombone is developed.

**1476** The first music books of plainsong are printed.

**c.1500** Muslims invade Indonesia and note that gamelan music has been around for centuries.

**1500s** The French chanson (song) becomes popular—it often told a story of lost love.

Italian musicians begin writing original music and introduce dynamics and orchestration.

In England Thomas Tallis writes many anthems, which become an important musical form.

In the Lutheran church the congregation joins in the singing, and hymns are in the local language (rather than Latin).

**1501** Ottaviano dei Petrucci publishes the first book of polyphonic music.

**c.1550s** The first *son* song is performed in Santiago, Chile.

**1558** Italian composer Gioseffo Zarlino publishes *Le istitutioni harmoniche*, which describes the use of chords in writing harmony.

**late 1500s** Music appears with specific parts for female singers.

Nicola Vincentino begins writing madrigals—songs for several unaccompanied voices.

**1594** Jacopo Peri composes *Dafne*, the first opera.

**1597** English composer John Dowland publishes four books of songs with lute accompaniment.

**1600** Dawn of the Baroque era.

**1600s** African slaves are brought to Europe and America, bringing their music with them.

Oratorios start to develop at religious meetings held by the Italian Filippo Neri.

Castrati are singing in operas.

**1620** Pilgrims arrive in America from Europe bringing their psalms and hymns with them.

**1685** Johann Sebastian Bach born in Germany.

**1689** The English opera *Dido and Aeneas* by Henry Purcell opens in London.

**early 1700s** Johann Christoff Denner invents the clarinet.

**1709** Bartolomeo Cristofori invents the pianoforte (the piano).

**1722** Bach publishes *The Well-tempered Clavichord*, a collection of keyboard pieces in all the major and minor keys.

**1727** The first German singspiel (*The Devil Is Loose*) is produced.

**1731** The first formal classical concert takes place in America.

**1742** The first performance of Handel's oratorio *Messiah*.

**1748** The first public concert hall opens in Oxford, England.

**c.1750** The Classical era begins.

**1756** Wolfgang Amadeus Mozart born in Salzburg, Austria.

**1770** William Billings publishes the first book of American music, *The New-England Psalm-Singer*.

Ludwig van Beethoven born in Bonn, Germany.

**1777** "Yankee Doodle" is the first American song published in Europe.

**1786** Mozart composes his opera *The Marriage of Figaro*.

**late 1700s** German composers start writing lieder, songs in which the lyrics are all-important.

**1790** The first performance of Peking (Beijing) opera.

**1791–1795** "Father of the symphony" Joseph Haydn writes his 12 "London" symphonies, including his *Surprise* Symphony.

**c.1800** Beethoven increases the size of the classical orchestra and ushers in the Romantic era.

The waltz grows in popularity throughout Europe.

**1800s** African-American slaves use Christian hymns as the basis for their own spirituals.

**early 1800s** Caribbean and African styles combine in Sierra Leone to create "highlife."

**1814** "The Star-Spangled Banner" is first performed.

**1823** Beethoven completes his Ninth Symphony.

**mid-1840s** Blackfaced minstrel shows become popular in America and Britain.

**1853** First performance of Verdi's opera *La Traviata*.

**c.1850s** The banjo becomes a popular instrument among gold miners in America.

European composers start writing nationalistic music.

**c.1860** Vienna, Austria, becomes the main center of operetta.

**1864** Adolphe Sax invents the saxophone.

**1871** Spirituals are first performed for a white audience by the Jubilee Singers.

**1876** Brahms completes his First Symphony.

First performance of Wagner's four-opera cycle *The Ring of the Nibelungen*.

**1877** First performance of Tchaikovsky's ballet *Swan Lake*.

**1878** David Edward Hughes invents the carbon microphone.

**1879** Bandleader Miguel Failde creates *danzón* dance music.

**late 1800s** Appalachian folk music is adapted into hillbilly—and later country—music.

Barbershop quartet singing becomes popular in America.

Millions of copies of sheet music are sold for people to play songs on their pianos at home.

African Americans start performing the blues.

**c.1890** Vaudeville becomes America's most popular form of mass entertainment.

**1891** Carnegie Hall opens in New York City.

**1894** First performance of the impressionist *Prélude à l'après-midi d'un faune* by Debussy.

Emil Berliner invents the gramophone and the record disk.

**1896** First performance of Puccini's opera *La Bohème*.

**1899** Scott Joplin's "Maple Leaf Rag" helps make ragtime popular.

**c.1900** Expressionist composers begin placing equal importance on all 12 semitones of the scale.

Mariachi bands begin performing in Mexico.

**early 1900s** In New Orleans African-American marching bands form the first jazz groups.

African Americans adapt "shout" songs and church "witness" rituals to make gospel.

Austrian composers Arnold Schoenberg and Alban Berg develop *Sprechgesang* singing.

**1901** Premiere of Rachmaninov's Second Piano Concerto.

**1902** Enrico Caruso makes recordings for the gramophone.

**1906** Béla Bartók begins recording Hungarian folk songs.

**1909** William Ludwig invents the foot pedal for the bass drum.

**c.1910** Tin Pan Alley starts producing popular songs.

**1911** Premiere of Richard Strauss's opera *Der Rosenkavalier*.

**1913** First performance in Paris of Stravinsky's *The Rite of Spring* causes a riot in the audience.

**1917** The Original Dixieland Jazz Band makes the first phonograph recordings of jazz tunes.

**1920** Léon Thérémin invents the "theremin," the first important electronic instrument.

Mamie Smith's "Crazy Blues" is the first blues recording featuring a black performer.

**1920–1923** Arnold Schoenberg writes his first pieces of serialist music, based on a tone row.

**1920s** The jazz age. Chicago replaces New Orleans as the center of jazz.

The first jug bands are formed.

The beginnings of electronic music.

*Enka*, combining Western music with traditional Japanese minor modes, develops in Japan.

Blues guitarists develop the slide technique of gliding the fingers up and down the strings instead of using the frets.

The amplifier is invented.

The tango becomes popular in America and Europe.

Dance-band singers start using the microphone.

Blues musicians start playing a "walking bass," which leads to boogie-woogie.

Muzak begins recording production (background) music.

Sheet-music sales decrease as record sales increase.

**1921** Prokofiev's opera *The Love for Three Oranges* first performed.

**1923** King Oliver's Creole Jazz Band, featuring Louis Armstrong on trumpet, makes the first jazz

recordings by an all-black group.

The first country record, Fiddlin' John Carson's "The Little Old Log Cabin in the Lane," is made in Atlanta, Georgia.

**1924** Premiere of George Gershwin's *Rhapsody in Blue*.

**1925** George Dewey Hay begins broadcasting a radio show—later known as *The Grand Ole Opry*—from Nashville, Tennessee.

**1926** Louis Armstrong invents "scat singing."

**1927** Premiere of the first modern musical—Jerome Kern and Oscar Hammerstein II's *Show Boat*.

The first motion picture with sound is *The Jazz Singer*.

**1928** Joe Falcon's "Allons a Lafayette" is the first Cajun record.

Kurt Weill and Bertolt Brecht's musical *The Threepenny Opera* includes political satire.

**1930s** "Swing"—African-American dance music—becomes popular.

Folk singer Woody Guthrie sings songs about the Depression.

**1934** The Hammond organ is invented by Laurens Hammond.

Magnetic recording tape is developed.

**1935** The electric guitar and the tape recorder are invented.

**1938** Mambo music begins in Cuba.

**1940s** Latin music begins to influence American jazz.

Big-band singers Ella Fitzgerald, Peggy Lee, and Frank Sinatra embark on solo careers.

Bebop emerges as improvisational jazz music.

**1943–1959** Rodgers and Hammerstein write a string of successful musicals.

**1944** Premiere of Aaron Copland's ballet *Appalachian Spring*.

**late 1940s** Dance "race music" becomes "rhythm and blues."

*Musique concrète* is used in orchestral compositions.

The electric piano is invented.

**1948** The long-playing 33⅓ record (the LP) is introduced.

**1949** "Father of honky-tonk" Hank Williams has first big hit with "Lovesick Blues."

Miles Davis releases *Birth of the Cool*, the first "cool jazz" record.

**1950s** Leo Fender designs the Telecaster and the Stratocaster electric guitars.

A new music called bossa nova emerges from Brazil—a light jazz sound with samba and *choro* influences.

Young African Americans start singing doo-wop.

"Soul" emerges, adapted from the gospel sound.

Technological advances include tape recording and stereo.

**1951** Elliot Carter composes his atonal String Quartet No. 1.

**1952** Pierre Boulez composes his serialist piece *Structures I*.

John Cage performs his experimental piece *4' 33"*.

**1953** Enrique Jorrin invents the cha-cha-cha.

**mid-1950s** DJ Alan Freed coins the term "rock 'n' roll."

**1955** The first synthesizer is built.

**1956** Elvis Presley reaches No. 1 with the rock 'n' roll song "Heartbreak Hotel."

Frank Sinatra releases *Songs for Swinging Lovers*.

**1959** Stockhausen performs his aleatory piece *Zyklus*.

Miles Davis abandons cool in favor of modal jazz.

Rock 'n' roll star Buddy Holly is killed in a place crash.

Berry Gordy and Smokey Robinson start Motown Records.

**1960** The Shirelles become the first black girl group to have a No. 1 hit single.

Saxophonist Ornette Coleman starts a new improvisational jazz sound called "free jazz."

**1960s** Period performances of Baroque pieces become popular.

The Andean music known as *chicha* is developed.

**1962** The Beatles make their first record, "Love Me Do."

**1963** "Queen of Country" Patsy Cline dies in a plane crash.

Bob Dylan records the 1960s folk anthem "Blowin' in the Wind."

**1965** James Brown introduces a new style of dance music, "funk."

Folk rock begins when Bob Dylan plays an electric guitar instead of an acoustic one at the Newport Jazz Festival.

The analog synthesizer is made available to the public.

**late 1960s** Some bands begin playing psychedelic rock.

Progressive rock emerges.

**1967** Digital recording technology is developed.

The Beatles release *Sgt. Pepper's Lonely Hearts Club Band*.

**1968** Steppenwolf's "Born to Be Wild" is first heavy metal record.

Country singer Johnny Cash releases *Live at Folsom Prison*.

**1969** Miles Davis combines free jazz and rock to form "fusion."

**1970s** Indian music becomes popular in the West.

Salsa becomes a popular type of Latin-based dance music.

Jamaica's reggae begins to spread around the world.

**mid-1970s** Disco music becomes popular.

**1976** Punk rock band the Sex Pistols sends shock waves across Britain with "Anarchy in the U.K."

**late 1970s** The DJ-led hip-hop begins among the black urban youth of America.

**1979** Ry Cooder's album *Bop till You Drop* is the first to use a digital multitrack system.

**1980s** Cajun music enjoys a national revival.

Digital recording becomes available.

The introduction of CDs transforms the music industry.

**1981** MTV begins broadcasting on cable and satellite.

**1983** MIDI (Musical Instrument Digital Interface) enables two or more electronic instruments to communicate with each other.

**1986** Ladysmith Black Mambazo from South Africa introduces Zulu a capella music to the world.

**1987** Premiere of John Adams' minimalist opera *Nixon in China*.

**1990s** Digital sampling becomes more common in pop music.

**1996** In the violent world of gangsta rap, Tupac Shakur is shot dead in Las Vegas.

**late 1990s** Hospitals and clinics begin using music therapy.

Internet users begin downloading music onto their personal computers.

# Glossary

**anthem** A vocal composition usually with moral or religious **lyrics**, a series of verses, and a powerful **chorus**.

**arrangement** A composition rewritten or adapted for different instruments.

**avant-garde** A term used to describe an artist or art form using radical or innovative techniques.

**backbeat** A style of drumming that emphasizes the second and fourth beats of a four-beat **rhythm**.

**ballad** Either a song telling a story or a slow, sentimental song.

**blues** A traditional African-American music that influenced all forms of popular music in the 20th century, particularly jazz and **R&B**. Originally an emotional voice and guitar- or piano-based music, it came to define a form based on repeated sections of 12 bars (measures) each. After four bars the piece moves to a series of set keys before changing back to the original key for the final two bars.

**call-and-response** A style of music derived from the work songs of slaves, in which a solo cry was answered with a response from the rest of the workers.

**calypso** A Trinidadian style of **ballad** originating in the 19th century with bouncy **rhythms** and **lyrics** that make a political or social comment.

**chord** Three or more notes that are sounded at the same time.

**choreographer** A person who arranges dance movements for ballets or other dance performances.

**chorus** The section of a song that comes after the verse and is usually repeated again at the end of each verse. Also an organized group of singers, usually of nonchurch music.

**cross-rhythms** Conflicting **rhythms**, such as a three-beat rhythm played against a two-beat rhythm.

**disco** An upbeat dance music popular in the 1970s, created for discotheques.

**doo-wop** A music style that originated in the 1930s and peaked in the 1950s, usually featuring unaccompanied four-part **harmony** singing by vocal groups using nonsense words.

**dub** A type of **reggae** most popular in the 1970s in which the producer takes out everything but drums and bass, treats them with echo effects, and mixes the vocals in and out.

**flat** A symbol indicating that a note's **pitch** be lowered by one **semitone**.

**frets** Thin strips of wood, metal, or ivory on a stringed instrument's fingerboard that mark the points where fingers are placed to sound the notes.

**funk/funky** A danceable style of **R&B** that emphasizes the first and third beats of a bar (measure). It originated with James Brown in the 1960s and became extremely popular in the 1970s.

**gangsta rap** An aggressive style of **rap** with **lyrics** that talk about ghetto city life and the violence encountered there.

**goombay** A Bahamian genre mixing traditional African and European styles. It was usually played using a *goombay* drum made of goatskin, a saw scraped by a metal file, maracas, rhythm sticks, and a bass violin made from a washtub, string, and a three-foot stick.

**grunge** A mixture of **heavy metal** and punk that became popular in the late 1980s and throughout the 1990s.

**harmony** Two or more notes sounding together in a "harmonious," or complementary, way.

**heavy metal** A loud, direct style of rock music that uses powerful guitar **chord** progressions and riffs over forceful bass and drums. It began in the late 1960s and is still popular today.

**hymn** A song of praise to God, usually written for church services.

**improvise/improvisation** Creating music spontaneously, without planning what is going to be played or sung.

**interlude** Instrumental music played between acts of a play or opera.

**interval** The distance in **pitch** between two notes.

**lambada** A type of dance music that originated in the 1960s in northern Brazil and combined **merengue**, salsa, and **reggae**. It became an international dance craze in the 1990s.

**lineup** The instruments used in a group or band.

**lyrics** The words of a song.

**major** The term used for **intervals**, **chords**, and **scales** that use the major third and sixth (see page 72).

**march** A piece of music with a regular **rhythm** played by military bands to help soldiers keep in step.

**mazurka** A Polish folk dance written in 3/4 time (counted as 1-2-3, 1-2-3).

**merengue** A Dominican style of dance music played on accordion, brass, and percussion instruments.

**méringue** A slower Haitian variation of Dominican **merengue** that uses guitar instead of accordion.

**minor** The term used for **intervals**, **chords**, and **scales** that use the minor, or flattened, third and sixth (see page 72).

**minuet** A French country dance in 3/4 time (counted as 1-2-3, 1-2-3).

**mode** One of a series of **scales** created by the ancient Greeks and adopted by the Christian church in medieval times. They are still used in some modern forms of music, such as folk and jazz. Some of the most common modes in Western music are the Phrygian, the Dorian, and the Ionian.

**modulation** Changing from one key to another in a musical composition.

**octave** The eighth note up or down from any other note. Also the **interval** between these two notes.

**orchestration** The assigning of parts to specific instruments of an orchestra.

**phonograph** An early term for a device that reproduced recorded sound.

**pick** A small, thin object made of a strong but flexible material that is held between the fingers to pluck the strings of an instrument and create a sound.

**pitch** The sound quality of a note that is determined by the frequency of the vibrations producing the note.

**polka** A lively Eastern European dance in 2/4 time (counted as 1-2, 1-2) that originated around 1830.

**polyrhythms** Two or more rhythms that are played simultaneously.

**psychedelic** A style of rock music associated with hallucinogenic drugs that originated in the late 1960s. It has long, **improvised** instrumental passages and uses sound effects like echo.

**quarter-tone** An interval that is equal to one-half of a **semitone**.

**rap** An African-American music style begun in New York in the 1970s with

syncopated, rhyming **lyrics** spoken or half-sung over **rhythmic** music.

**reggae** A Jamaican music style of the 1970s with **lyrics** connected to the Rastafarian religion, catchy melodies, and a **syncopated** beat. It combines the **rhythms** of **rock steady** with a slower version of **ska**. Its biggest star was Bob Marley, and it is still a vital force in rock, pop, **rap**, and **rhythm and blues**.

**resonator** The part of an instrument that increases the sound by resonating.

**rhythm/rhythmic** The underlying pulse or beat of the music.

**rhythm and blues (R&B)** African-American music style that began in the late 1930s as "race music" and became known as rhythm and blues in 1949. It has repetitive upbeat **rhythms** and simple **harmonies** and melodies that use elements of the **blues**. When white artists recorded it, it was called "rock 'n' roll." By the late 1960s much rhythm and blues became known as "soul." In the 1990s the term was used to describe the smooth pop music of artists like Jodeci and R. Kelly.

**rock steady** A 1960s Jamaican music that evolved from **ska** and into **reggae**. It is less jazzy than ska, with prominent bass lines and guitars playing steady off-beat **rhythms**—hence its name.

**rumba** A Cuban dance and music style based on a **syncopated** African rhythm that is usually played on drums or an instrument called the clave (two wooden blocks). Other percussion instruments add **cross-rhythms** or **polyrhythms**, while a lead singer and **chorus** sing in a back-and-forth pattern known as "call-and-response."

**samba** A lively Brazilian music style based on a relaxed 2/4 beat (counted as 1-2, 1-2) overlaid with powerful **syncopated rhythms**.

**scale** A series of (usually) eight notes ascending or descending in alphabetical order and in specified **intervals** (whole-tones or half-tones).

**semitone** One of the 12 half-tones in an **octave**.

**sharp** A symbol indicating that a note's **pitch** be raised by one **semitone**.

**ska** An early form of Jamaican **reggae** with a faster shuffling rhythm.

**son** A Cuban music style from the 16th century that mixes the clave **rhythm** of **rumba** with Spanish guitar rhythms.

**swing** A style of dance music popular in the 1930s and 1940s.

**syncopation** A way of making the accent of the **rhythm** fall on the normally unaccented or weaker beats of a bar.

**tempo** The speed at which a musical piece is played, whether fast or slow.

**tenor** The highest normal adult male singing voice.

**tone color** The sound quality of a voice or instrument.

**tuning** Changing the **pitch** of a note on an instrument to a standard or especially chosen pitch.

**vibrato** The consistent fluttering of a note at a **pitch** higher or lower than the main note.

**virtuoso** A musician of exceptional technical skill.

**waltz** A dance music style in 3/4 time (counted as 1-2-3, 1-2-3) that originated in the late 18th century.

**world music** A term used by record companies to describe any music that is not a major Western music style.

# Musical Notation

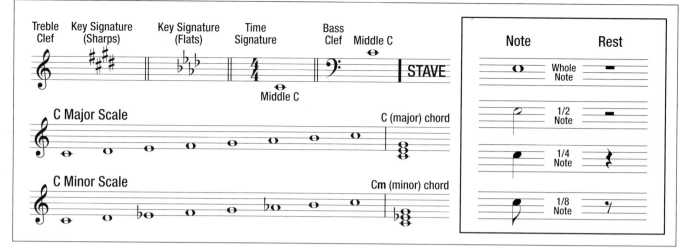

# Further Reading

Barber, Nicola, and Mary Mure with Carl Melegari (illustrator). *The World of Music*. Ontario, Canada: Silver Burdett Press, 1995.

Bergamini, Andrea. *Music of the World* (Masters of Music). Hauppage, NY: Barron's Juveniles, 1999.

Boullier, Diann. *Exploring Irish Music and Dance*. Niwot, CO: Irish American Book Company, 1998.

Brunning, Bob. *Reggae*. Lincolnwood, IL: NTC Publishing Group, 1999.

Chang, Kevin O'Brien, and Wayne Chen. *Reggae Roots: The Story of Jamaican Music*. Philadelphia, PA: Temple University Press, 1998.

*Christmas in Brazil* (World Book). New York: World Book, 1998.

Decesare, Ruth, with John O'Reilly and Patrick Wilson (editors). *Songs of Hispanic America*. Van Nuys, CA: Alfred Publishing Company, 2000.

Donahoe, Kitty, with Pasqua C. Warstler (illustrator). *Bunyan and Banjoes: Michigan Songs and Stories* (Volume I with cassette). San Diego, CA: Thunder Bay Press, 1997.

Doney, Meryl. *Musical Instruments* (World Crafts). Danbury, CT: Franklin Watts, 1997.

Ewens, Graeme. *Africa O-Ye: A Celebration of African Music*. New York: Da Capo Press, 1992.

Fradin, Dennis Brindell. *Ethiopia*. Danbury, CT: Children's Press, 1997.

Gilfoyle, Millie. *Bob Marley*. Broomall, PA: Chelsea House Publishers, 1999.

Hasday, Judy L. *Musical Instruments from around the World*. Broomall, PA: Chelsea House Publishers, 1999.

Imoto, Yoko. *Best-Loved Children's Songs from Japan*. Torrance, CA: Heian International Publishing, 1996.

Jensen, Anne Ferguson. *India: Its Culture and People*. Upper Saddle River, NJ: Longman Publishing Group, 1991.

Kalman, Bobbie D. *China: The Culture*. New York: Crabtree Publishing Company, 1995.

Kalman, Bobbie D. *India: The Culture*. New York: Crabtree Publishing Company, 1995.

Laufer, Peter, with Susan L. Roth (illustrator). *Made in Mexico*. Berkeley, CA: National Geographic Society, 2000.

Livo, Norma J. (editor). *Troubadour's Storybag: Musical Folktales of the World*. Golden, CO: Fulcrum Publishing, 1996.

Lodge, Bernard (illustrator). *Songs for Survival: Songs and Chants from Tribal Peoples around the World*. New York: Penguin Putnam Books for Young Readers, 1996.

Lottridge, Celia Barker. *Music for the Tsar of the Sea*. Berkeley, CA: Groundwood-Douglas & McIntyre, 1998.

Silverman, Jerry. *African Roots*. Broomall, PA: Chelsea House Publishers, 1993.

Silverman, Jerry. *West Indian and Calypso Songs*. Broomall, PA: Chelsea House Publishers, 1994.

Stein, Heather Conrad. *Cultures of the Past: Set 1*. Tarrytown, NY: Marshall Cavendish, 1996.

Tate, Carole. *Rhymes and Ballads of London*. Merrick, NY: Scroll Press, 1973.

Toouma, Habib Hassan. *The Music of the Arabs*. Portland, OR: Amadeus Press, 1996.

## Useful websites

*The African Music Encyclopedia* (a country-by-country database of African musicians and styles)
http://www.africanmusic.org

*Arabic Music Information Source* (includes downloadable clips of Arabic music)
http://members.aol.com/amisource

*BrazilianMusic.com* (includes profiles of key Brazilian musicians)
http://www.brazilianmusic.com

*Fun World Music Facts* (humorous site)
http://www.wfmu.org/Playlists/Robw/funfax.html

*International Music Archives* (covers music from all over the world)
http://www.eyeneer.com/World/index.html

*Middle Eastern Culture* (includes downloadable clips of all forms of Middle Eastern music)
http://www.shira.net/culture.htm

*Ravi Shankar Foundation* (explores Indian classical music)
http://www.ravishankar.org

*Rootsworld* (online magazine dedicated to traditional music from around the world)
http://www.rootsworld.com

*Salsaweb* (news about current salsa stars)
http://www.salsaweb.com

# Set Index